THE BEST LOVED POEMS
AND BALLADS OF
JAMES WHITCOMB RILEY

THE
BEST LOVED POEMS
and BALLADS *of*
James Whitcomb Riley

OMNIBUS EDITION

With Illustrations by
ETHEL FRANKLIN BETTS

BLUE RIBBON BOOKS, INC.
NEW YORK CITY

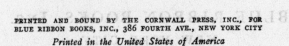

PRINTED AND BOUND BY THE CORNWALL PRESS, INC., FOR
BLUE RIBBON BOOKS, INC., 386 FOURTH AVE., NEW YORK CITY
Printed in the United States of America

To

The Children of The Old Times and of These

With changeless love

WHILE THE HEART BEATS YOUNG

WHILE the heart beats young!—O the
  splendor of the Spring,
With all her dewy jewels on, is not so fair a
  thing!
The fairest, rarest morning of the blossom-time
  of May
Is not so sweet a season as the season of to-day
While Youth's diviner climate folds and holds us,
  close caressed,
As we feel our mothers with us by the touch of
  face and breast;—
Our bare feet in the meadows, and our fancies
  up among
The airy clouds of morning—while the heart
  beats young.

While the heart beats young and our pulses leap
  and dance,
With every day a holiday and life a glad
  romance,—
We hear the birds with wonder, and with wonder
  watch their flight—
Standing still the more enchanted, both of
  hearing and of sight,

When they have vanished wholly,—for, in fancy,
    wing-to-wing
We fly to Heaven with them; and, returning,
    still we sing
The praises of this lower Heaven with tireless
    voice and tongue,
Even as the Master sanctions—while the heart
    beats young.

While the heart beats young!—While the heart
    beats young!
O green and gold old Earth of ours, with azure
    overhung
And looped with rainbows!—grant us yet this
    grassy lap of thine—
We would be still thy children, through the shower
    and the shine!
So pray we, lisping, whispering, in childish love
    and trust,
With our beseeching hands and faces lifted from
    the dust
By fervor of the poem, all unwritten and unsung,
Thou givest us in answer, while the heart beats
    young.

CONTENTS

CONTENTS—CONTINUED

CONTENTS—CONTINUED

CONTENTS—CONTINUED

CONTENTS—CONTINUED

CONTENTS—CONTINUED

CONTENTS—CONTINUED

CONTENTS—CONTINUED

CONTENTS—CONTINUED

CONTENTS—CONTINUED

THE BEST LOVED POEMS
AND BALLADS OF
JAMES WHITCOMB RILEY

THE RAGGEDY MAN

O THE RAGGEDY MAN! He works fer **Pa**;
   An' he's the goodest man ever you saw!
   He comes to our house every day,
An' waters the horses, an' feeds 'em hay;
An' he opens the shed—an' we all ist laugh
When he drives out our little old wobble-ly calf;
An' nen—ef our hired girl says he can—
He milks the cow fer 'Lizabuth Ann.—
   Ain't he a' awful good Raggedy Man?
   Raggedy! Raggedy! Raggedy Man!

W'y, The Raggedy Man—he's ist so good
He splits the kindlin' an' chops the wood;
An' nen he spades in our garden, too,
An' does most things 'at *boys* can't do!—
He clumbed clean up in our big tree
An' shooked a' apple down fer me—
An' nother'n', too, fer 'Lizabuth Ann—
An' nother'n', too, fer The Raggedy Man.—
  Ain't he a' awful kind Raggedy Man?
    Raggedy! Raggedy! Raggedy Man!

An' The Raggedy Man, he knows most rhymes
An' tells 'em, ef I be good, sometimes:
Knows 'bout Giuhts, an' Griffuns, an' Elves,
An' the Squidgicum-Squees 'at swallers therselves!
An', wite by the pump in our pasture-lot,
He showed me the hole 'at the Wunks is got,
'At lives 'way deep in the ground, an' can
Turn into me, er 'Lizabuth Ann,
Er Ma er Pa er The Raggedy Man!
  Ain't he a funny old Raggedy Man?
    Raggedy! Raggedy! Raggedy Man!

The Raggedy Man—one time when he
Wuz makin' a little bow-'n'-orry fer me,
Says "When *you're* big like your Pa is,
Air *you* go' to keep a fine store like his—
An' be a rich merchunt—an' wear fine clothes?—
Er what *air* you go' to be, goodness knows!"
An' nen he laughed at 'Lizabuth Ann,
An' I says " 'M go' to be a Raggedy Man!—
   I'm ist go' to be a nice Raggedy Man!"
     Raggedy! Raggedy! Raggedy Man!

WHERE SHALL WE LAND

Where shall we land you, sweet?
                                    —Swinburne

ALL listlessly we float
        Out seaward in the boat
        That beareth Love.
Our sails of purest snow
Bend to the blue below
    And to the blue above.
        Where shall we land?

We drift upon a tide
Shoreless on every side,
    Save where the eye
Of Fancy sweeps far lands
Shelved slopingly with sands
    Of gold and porphyry.
        Where shall we land?

The fairy isles we see,
Loom up so mistily—
    So vaguely fair,
We do not care to break
Fresh bubbles in our wake
    To bend our course for there.
        Where shall we land?

The warm winds of the deep
Have lulled our sails to sleep,
   And so we glide
Careless of wave or wind,
Or change of any kind,
   Or turn of any tide.
      Where shall we land?

We droop our dreamy eyes
Where our reflection lies
   Steeped in the sea,
And, in an endless fit
Of languor, smile on it
   And its sweet mimicry.
      Where shall we land?

"Where shall we land?" God's grace!
I know not any place
   So fair as this—
Swung here between the blue
Of sea and sky, with you
   To ask me, with a kiss,
      "Where shall we land?"

MAYMIE'S STORY OF RED RIDING-HOOD

W'Y, one time wuz a little-weenty dirl,
    An' she wuz named Red Riding-Hood,
      'cause her—
Her *Ma* she maked a little red cloak fer her
'At turnt up over her head.—An' it 'uz all
Ist one piece o' red cardinul 'at's like
The drate-long stockin's the storekeepers has.—
Oh! it 'uz purtiest cloak in all the world
An' *all* this town er anywheres they is!
An' so, one day, her Ma she put it on
Red Riding-Hood, she did—one day, she did —
An' it 'uz *Sund'y*—'cause the little cloak
It 'uz too nice to wear ist *ever'* day
An' *all* the time!—An' so her Ma, she put
It on Red Riding-Hood—an' telled her not
To dit no dirt on it ner dit it mussed
Ner nothin'! An'—an'—nen her Ma she dot

Her little basket out, 'at Old Kriss bringed
Her wunst—one time, he did. An' nen she fill'
It full o' whole lots an' 'bundance o' dood things **t' eat**
(Allus my Dran'ma *she* says " 'bundance," too).
An' so her Ma fill' little Red Riding-Hood's
Nice basket all ist full o' dood things t' eat,
An' tell her take 'em to her old Dran'ma—
An' not to *spill* 'em, neever—'cause ef she
'Ud stump her toe an' spill 'em, her Dran'ma
She'll haf to *punish* her!

                                 An' nen—An' so
Little Red Riding-Hood she p'omised she
'Ud be all careful nen, an' cross' her heart
'At she won't run an' spill 'em all fer six—
Five—ten—two-hundred-bushel-dollars-gold!
An' nen she kiss' her Ma doo'-by an' went
A-skippin' off—away fur off frough the
Big woods, where her Dran'ma she live at—
     No!—
She didn't do *a-skippin'*, like I said:—
She ist went *walkin'*—careful-like an' slow—
Ist like a little lady—walkin' 'long
As all polite an' nice—an' slow—an' straight—
An' turn her toes—ist like she's marchin' in
The Sund'y-School k-session!
                              An'—an'—so
She 'uz a-doin' along—an' doin' along—

On frough the drate-big woods—'cause her
    Dran'ma
She live 'way, 'way fur off frough the big woods
From *her* Ma's house. So when Red Riding-Hood
Dit to do there, she allus have most fun—
When she do frough the drate-big woods, you
    know.—
'Cause she ain't feard a bit o' anything!
An' so she sees the little hoppty-birds
'At's in the trees, an' flyin' all around,
An' singin' dlad as ef their parunts said
They'll take 'em to the magic-lantern show!
An' she 'ud pull the purty flowers an' things
A-growin' round the stumps.—An' she 'ud ketch
The purty butterflies, an' drasshoppers,
An' stick pins frough 'em—No!—I ist *said* that!—
'Cause she's too dood an' kind an' 'bedient
To *hurt* things thataway.—She'd *ketch* 'em, though,
An' ist *play* wiv 'em ist a little while,
An' nen she'd let 'em fly away, she would,
An' ist skip on ad'in to her Dran'ma's.

An' so, while she 'uz doin' 'long an' 'long,
First thing you know they 'uz a drate-big old
Mean wicked Wolf jumped out 'at wanted t' eat
Her up, but *dassent* to—'cause wite clos't there
They wuz a Man a-choppin' wood, an' you

Could *hear* him.—So the old Wolf he 'uz *feard*
Only to ist be *kind* to her.—So he
Ist 'tended-like he wuz dood friends to her
An' says, "Dood morning, little Red Riding-
        Hood!"—
All ist as kind!
                    An' nen Riding-Hood
She say "Dood morning," too—all kind an' nice—
Ist like her Ma she learn'—No!—mustn't say
"Learn'," 'cause *"learn'"* it's unproper.—So she say
It like her *Ma* she *"teached"* her.—An'—so she
Ist says "Dood morning" to the Wolf—'cause she
Don't know ut-tall 'at he's a *wicked* Wolf
An' want to eat her up!
                    Nen old Wolf smile
An' say, so kind: "Where air you doin' at?"
Nen little Red Riding-Hood she say: "I'm doin'
To my Dran'ma's, 'cause my Ma say I might."
Nen, when she tell him that, the old Wolf he
Ist turn an' light out frough the big thick woods,
Where she can't see him any more. An' so
She think he's went to *his* house—but he hain't,—
He's went to her Dran'ma's, to be there first—
An' *ketch* her, ef she don't watch mighty sharp
What she's about!

An' nen when the old Wolf
Dit to her Dran'ma's house, he's purty smart, —
An' so he 'tend-like *he's* Red Riding-Hood,
An' knock at th' door. An' Riding-Hood's Dran'ma
She's sick in bed an' can't come to the door
An' open it. So th' old Wolf knock' *two* times.
An' nen Red Riding-Hood's Dran'ma she says,
"Who's there?" she says. An' old Wolf 'tends-like
      he's
Little Red Riding-Hood, you know, an' make'
His voice soun' ist like hers, an' says: "It's me,
Dran'ma—an' I'm Red Riding-Hood an' I'm
Ist come to *see* you."
                              Nen her old Dran'ma
She think it *is* little Red Riding-Hood,
An' so she say: "Well, come in nen an' make
You'se'f at home," she says, " 'cause I'm down sick
In bed, an' got the 'ralgia, so's I can't
Dit up an' let ye in."
                          An' so th' old Wolf
Ist march' in nen an' shet the door ad'in,
An' *drowl'*, he did, an' *splunge'* up on the bed
An' et up old Miz Riding-Hood 'fore she
Could put her specs on an' see who it wuz.—
An' so she never knowed *who* et her up!

28

'An' nen the wicked Wolf he ist put on
Her nightcap, an' all covered up in bed—
Like he wuz *her,* you know.

                Nen, purty soon
Here come along little Red Riding-Hood,
An' *she* knock' at the door. An' old Wolf 'tend-
Like *he's* her Dran'ma; an' he say, "Who's there?"
Ist like her Dran'ma say, you know. An' so
Little Red Riding-Hood she say: "It's *me,*
Dran'ma—an' I'm Red Riding-Hood an' I'm
Ist come to *see* you."

              An' nen old Wolf nen
He cough an' say: "Well, come in nen an' make
You'se'f at home," he says, " 'cause I'm down sick
In bed, an' got the 'ralgia, so's I can't
Dit up an' let ye in."

              An' so she think
It's her Dran'ma a-talkin'.—So she ist
Open' the door an' come in, an' set down
Her basket, an' taked off her things, an' bringed
A chair an' clumbed up on the bed, wite by
The old big Wolf she thinks is her Dran'ma—
Only she thinks the old Wolf's dot whole lots
More bigger ears, an' lots more whiskers, too,
Than her Dran'ma; an' so Red Riding-Hood
She's kind o' skeered a little. So she says,

"Oh, Dran'ma, what *big eyes* you dot!" An' nen
The old Wolf says: "They're ist big thataway
'Cause I'm so dlad to see you!"

Nen she says,
"Oh, Dran'ma, what a drate-big nose you dot!"
Nen th' old Wolf says: "It's ist big thataway
Ist 'cause I smell the dood things 'at you bringed
Me in the basket!"

An' nen Riding-Hood
She says, "Oh-me-oh-*my!* Dran'ma! what big
White long sharp teeth you dot!"

Nen old Wolf says:
"Yes—an' they're thataway"—an' drowled—
"They're thataway," he says, "to *eat* you wiv!"
An' nen he ist *jump'* at her.—

But she *scream'*—
An' *scream',* she did.—So's 'at the Man
'At wuz a-choppin' wood, you know,—*he* hear,
An' come a-runnin' in there wiv his ax;
An', 'fore the old Wolf know' what he's about,
He split his old brains out an' killed him s' quick
It make' his head swim!—An' Red Riding-Hood
She wuzn't hurt at all!

An' the big Man
He tooked her all safe home, he did, an' tell
Her Ma she's all right an' ain't hurt at all

An' old Wolf's dead an' killed—an' ever'thing!—
So her Ma wuz so tickled an' so proud,
She gived *him* all the dood things t' eat they **wuz**
'At's in the basket, an' she tell' him 'at
She's much oblige', an' say to "call ad'in."
An' story's honest *truth*—an' all *so,* too!

A SUDDEN SHOWER

BAREFOOTED boys scud up the street,
　　Or skurry under sheltering sheds;
And schoolgirl faces, pale and sweet,
　　Gleam from the shawls about their heads.

Doors bang; and mother-voices call
　　From alien homes; and rusty gates
Are slammed; and high above it all,
　　The thunder grim reverberates.

And then, abrupt,—the rain! the rain!—
　　The earth lies gasping; and the eyes
Behind the streaming window-pane
　　Smile at the trouble of the skies.

The highway smokes; sharp echoes ring;
  The cattle bawl and cowbells clank;
And into town comes galloping
  The farmer's horse, with steaming flank.

The swallow dips beneath the eaves,
  And flirts his plumes and folds his wings;
And under the catawba leaves
  The caterpillar curls and clings.

The bumble-bee is pelted down
  The wet stem of the hollyhock;
And sullenly, in spattered brown,
  The cricket leaps the garden walk.

Within, the baby claps his hands
  And crows with rapture strange and vague;
Without, beneath the rosebush stands
  A dripping rooster on one leg.

THE USED-TO-BE

BEYOND the purple, hazy trees
    Of summer's utmost boundaries;
    Beyond the sands—beyond the seas—
Beyond the range of eyes like these,
  And only in the reach of the
  Enraptured gaze of Memory,
  There lies a land, long lost to me,—
    The land of Used-to-be!

A land enchanted—such as swung
In golden seas when sirens clung
Along their dripping brinks, and sung
To Jason in that mystic tongue
  That dazed men with its melody—
  O such a land, with such a sea
  Kissing its shores eternally,
    Is the fair Used-to-be.

A land where music ever girds
The air with belts of singing-birds,
And sows all sounds with such sweet words,
That even in the low of herds
  A meaning lives so sweet to me,
  Lost laughter ripples limpidly
  From lips brimmed over with the glee
    Of rare old Used-to-be.

Lost laughter, and the whistled tunes
Of boyhood's mouth of crescent runes,
That rounded, through long afternoons,
To serenading plenilunes—
  When starlight fell so mistily
  That, peering up from bended knee,
  I dreamed 'twas bridal drapery
    Snowed over Used-to-be.

O land of love and dreamy thoughts,
And shining fields, and shady spots
Of coolest, greenest grassy plots,
Embossed with wild forget-me-nots!—
  And all ye blooms that longingly
  Lift your fair faces up to me
  Out of the past, I kiss in ye
    The lips of Used-to-be.

CHRISTINE'S SONG

UP in Tentoleena Land—
      Tentoleena! Tentoleena!
'All the Dollies, hand in hand,
      Mina, Nainie, and Serena,
Dance the Fairy fancy dances,
With glad songs and starry glances,
Lisping roundelays; and, after,
Bird-like interludes of laughter
Strewn and scattered o'er the lawn
Their gilt sandals twinkle on
Through light mists of silver sand—
      Up in Tentoleena Land.

Up in Tentoleena Land—
        Tentoleena! Tentoleena!
Blares the eerie Elfin band—
        Trumpet, harp and concertina—
Larkspur bugle—honeysuckle
Cornet, with a quickstep chuckle
In its golden throat; and, maybe,
Lilies-of-the-valley they be
Baby-silver-bells that chime
Musically all the time,
Tossed about from hand to hand—
        Up in Tentoleena Land.

Up in Tentoleena Land—
        Tentoleena! Tentoleena!
Dollies dark, and blonde and bland—
        Sweet as musk-rose or verbena—
Sweet as moon-blown daffodillies,
        Or wave-jostled water-lilies,
Yearning to'rd the rose-mouths, ready
Leaning o'er the river's eddy,—
Dance, and glancing fling to you,
Through these lines you listen to,
Kisses blown from lip and hand
        Out of Tentoleena Land!

BUB SAYS

THE moon in the sky is a custard-pie,
　　An' the clouds is the cream pour'd o'er it,
An' all o' the glittering stars in the sky
　　Is the powdered sugar for it.

Johnts—he's proudest boy in town—
'Cause his Mommy she cut down
His Pa's pants fer Johnts—an' there
Is 'nuff left fer *'nother* pair!

One time, when her Ma was gone,
Little Elsie she put on
All her Ma's fine clothes—an' black
Grow-grain-silk, an' sealskin-sack;
Nen while she wuz flouncin' out
In the hall an' round about
Some one knocked, an' Elsie she
Clean forgot an' run to see
Who's there at the door—an' saw
Mighty quick at wuz her Ma.
But ef she ain't saw at all,
She'd a-knowed her parasol!

. . . .

Gran'pas an' Gran'mas is funniest folks!—
Don't be jolly, ner tell no jokes,
Tell o' the weather an' frost an' snow
O' that cold New Year's o' long ago;
And then they sigh at each other an' cough
An' talk about suddently droppin' off.

THE LISPER

ELSIE MINGUS *lisps*, she does!
  She lives wite acrosst from us
    In Miz. Ayers'uz house 'at she
Rents part to the Mingusuz.—
  Yes, an' Elsie plays wiv me.

Elsie lisps so, she can't say
Her own name, ist *anyway!*—
  She says *"Elthy"*—like they wuz
Feathers on her words, an' they
  Ist stick on her tongue like fuzz.

My! she's *purty,* though!—An' when
She *lisps,* w'y, she's purty *nen!*
  When she telled me, wunst, her doll
Wuz so "thweet," an' I p'ten'
  I lisp, too,—she laugh'—'at 's all!—

She don't never git mad none—
'Cause she know I'm ist in fun.—
   Elsie she ain't one bit sp'iled.—
Of all childerns—ever' one—
   She's the *ladylikest* child!—

My Ma *say* she is! One time
Elsie start to say the rhyme,
   "Thing a thong o' thixpenth"—*Whee!*
I ist *yell!* An' Ma say I'm
   Unpolite as I can be!

Wunst I went wiv Ma to call
On Elsie's Ma, an' eat an' all;
   An' nen Elsie, when we've et,
An' we 're playin' in the hall,
   Elsie say: It's etikett

Fer young gentlemens, like me,
Eatin' when they's *company,*
   Not to never ever crowd
Down their food, ner "thip their tea
   Ner thup thoop so awful loud!"

AT UTTER LOAF

I

AN afternoon as ripe with heat
    As might the golden pippin be
    With mellowness if at my feet
It dropped now from the apple-tree
My hammock swings in lazily.

II

The boughs about me spread a shade
    That shields me from the sun, but weaves
    With breezy shuttles through the leaves
Blue rifts of skies, to gleam and fade
    Upon the eyes that only see
    Just of themselves, all drowsily.

III

Above me drifts the fallen skein
    Of some tired spider, looped and blown,
As fragile as a strand of rain,
    Across the air, and upward thrown
    By breaths of hay-fields newly mown—
So glimmering it is and fine,
I doubt these drowsy eyes of mine.

42

IV

Far-off and faint as voices pent
  In mines, and heard from underground,
Come murmurs as of discontent,
  And clamorings of sullen sound
The city sends me, as, I guess,
To vex me, though they do but bless
Me in my drowsy fastnesses.

V

I have no care. I only know
  My hammock hides and holds me here
  In lands of shade a prisoner:
While lazily the breezes blow
  Light leaves of sunshine over me,
And back and forth and to and fro
  I swing, enwrapped in some hushed glee,
  Smiling at all things drowsily.

43

BUD'S FAIRY TALE

SOME peoples thinks they ain't no Fairies *now*
No more yet!—But they *is,* I bet! 'Cause ef
They *wuzn't* Fairies, nen I' like to know
Who'd w'ite 'bout Fairies in the books, an' tell
What Fairies *does,* an' how their *picture* looks,
An' all an' ever'thing! W'y, ef they don't
Be Fairies any more, nen little boys
'Ud ist *sleep* when they go to sleep an' won't
Have ist no dweams at all,—'cause Fairies—*good*
Fairies—they're a-purpose to make dweams!
But they *is* Fairies—an' I *know* they is!
'Cause one time wunst, when it's all Summer-time,
An' don't haf to be no fires in the stove
Er fireplace to keep warm wiv—ner don't haf
To wear old scwatchy flannen shirts at all,
An' ain't no fweeze—ner coid—ner snow!—An'—an'

44

Old skweeky twees got all the gween leaves on
An' ist keeps noddin', noddin' all the time,
Like they 'uz lazy an' a-twyin' to go
To sleep an' couldn't, 'cause the wind won't quit
A-blowin' in 'em, an' the birds won't stop
A-singin', so's they *kin*.—But twees *don't* sleep,
I guess! But *little boys* sleeps—an' *dweams,* too.—
An' that's a sign they's Fairies.

                              So, one time,
When I be'n playin' "Store" wunst over in
The shed of their old stable, an' Ed Howard
He maked me quit a-bein' pardners, 'cause
I dwinked the 'tend-like sody-water up
An' et the shore-'nuff crackers,—w'y, nen I
Clumbed over in our garden where the gwapes
Wuz purt' nigh ripe: An' I wuz ist a-layin'
There on th' old cwooked seat 'at Pa maked in
Our arber,—an' so I 'uz layin' there
A-whittlin' beets wiv my new dog-knife, an'
A-lookin' wite up thue the twimbly leaves—
An' wuzn't 'sleep at all!—An'-sir!—first thing
You know, a little *Fairy* hopped out there!—
A *leetle-teenty Fairy!—hope-may-die!*
An' he look' down at me, he did—an' he
Ain't bigger'n a *yellerbird!*—an' he
Say "Howdy-do!" he did—an' I could *hear*

Him—ist as *plain!*
Nen *I* say "Howdy-do!"

An' he say *"I'm* all hunky, Nibsey; how
Is *your* folks comin' on?"
An' nen I say

"My name ain't *'Nibsey,'* neever—my name's
    Bud.—
An' what's *your* name?" I says to him.
An' he

Ist laugh an' say, " *'Bud's'* awful *funny* name!"
An' he ist laid back on a big bunch o' gwapes
An' laugh' an' laugh', he did—like somebody
'Uz tick-el-un his feet!
An' nen I say—

"What's *your* name," nen I say, "afore you bu'st
Yo'se'f a-laughin' 'bout *my* name?" I says.
An' nen he dwy up laughin'—kind o' mad—
An' say, "W'y, *my* name's *Squidjicum,"* he says.
An' nen *I* laugh an' say—*"Gee!* what a name!"
An' when I make fun of his name, like that,
He ist git awful mad an' spunky, an'
'Fore you know, he gwabbed holt of a vine—
A big long vine 'at's danglin' up there, an'
He ist helt on wite tight to that, an' down
He swung quick past my face, he did, an' ist
Kicked at me hard's he could!

                                   But I'm too quick
Fer *Mr. Squidjicum!* I ist weached out
An' ketched him, in my hand—an' helt him, too,
An' *squeezed* him, ist like little wobins when
They can't fly yet an' git flopped out their nest.
An' nen I turn him all wound over, an'
Look at him clos't, you know—wite clos't,—'cause ef
He *is* a Fairy, w'y, I want to see
The *wings* he's got.—But he's dwessed up so fine
'At I can't *see* no wings.—An' all the time
He's twyin' to kick me yet: An' so I take
F'esh holts an' *squeeze* ag'in—an' harder, too;
An' I says, *"Hold up, Mr. Squidjicum!—*
You're kickin' the w'ong man!" I says; an' nen
I ist *squeeze'* him, purt' nigh my *best,* I did—
An' I heerd somepin' bu'st!—An' nen he cwied
An' says, "You better look out what you're doin'!—
You' bu'st my spider-web suspenners, an'
You' got my wose-leaf coat all cwinkled up
So's I can't go to old Miss Hoodjicum's
Tea-party, 's afternoon!"
                          An' nen I says —
"Who's 'old Miss Hoodjicum'?" I says.
                                        An' he
Says, "Ef you lemme loose I'll tell you."
                                          So
I helt the little skeezics 'way fur out

In one hand—so's he can't jump down t' th' ground
Wivout a-gittin' all stove up: an' nen
I says, "You're loose now.—Go ahead an' tell
'Bout the 'tea-party' where you're goin' at
So awful fast!" I says.

                          An' nen he say,—
"No use to *tell* you 'bout it, 'cause you won't
Believe it, 'less you go there your own se'f
An' see it wiv your own two eyes!" he says.
An' *he* says: "Ef you lemme *shore-'nuff* loose,
An' p'omise 'at you'll keep wite still, an' won't
Tetch nothin' 'at you see—an' never tell
Nobody in the world—an' lemme loose—
W'y, nen I'll *take* you there!"

                         But I says, "Yes
An' ef I let you loose, you'll *run!*" I says.
An' he says, "No, I won't!—I hope-may-die!"
Nen I says, "Cwoss your heart you won't!"

                                An' he
Ist cwoss his heart; an' nen I reach an' set
The little feller up on a long vine—
An' he 'uz so tickled to git loose ag'in,
He gwab the vine wiv boff his little hands
An' ist take an' turn in, he did, an' skin
'Bout forty-'leben cats!

                  Nen when he git

Thue whirlin' wound the vine, an' set on top
Of it ag'in, w'y, nen his "wose-leaf coat"
He bwag so much about, it's ist all tored
Up, an' ist hangin' strips an' rags—so he
Look like his Pa's a dwunkard. An' so nen
When he see what he's done—a-actin' up
So smart,—he's awful mad, I guess; an' ist
Pout out his lips an' twis' his little face
Ist ugly as he kin, an' set an' tear
His whole coat off—an' sleeves an' all.—An' nen
He wad it all togevver an' ist *th'ow*
It at me ist as hard as he kin dwive!

An' when I weach to ketch him, an' 'uz goin'
To give him 'nuvver squeezin', *he ist flewed*
Clean up on top the arbor!—'Cause, you know,
They *wuz* wings on him—when he tored his *coat*
Clean off—they *wuz* wings *under there*. But they
Wuz purty wobbly-like an' wouldn't work
Hardly at all—'cause purty soon, when I
Th'owed clods at him, an' sticks, an' got him shooed
Down off o' there, he come a-floppin' down
An' lit k-bang! on our old chicken-coop,
An' ist laid there a-whimper'n' like a child!
An' I tiptoed up wite clos't, an' I says, "What's
The matter wiv ye, Squidjicum?"

An' he
Says: "Dog-gone! when my wings gits stwaight
     ag'in,
Where you all *crumpled* 'em," he says, "I bet
I'll ist fly clean away an' won't take you
To old Miss Hoodjicum's at all!" he says.
An' nen I ist weach out wite quick, I did,
An' gwab the sassy little snipe ag'in—
Nen tooked my top-stwing an' tie down his wings
So's he *can't* fly, 'less'n I want him to!
An' nen I says: "Now, Mr. Squidjicum,
You better ist light out," I says, "to old
Miss Hoodjicum's, an' show *me* how to git
There, too," I says; "er ef you don't," I says,
"I'll climb up wiv you on our buggy-shed
An' push you off!" I says.
                                        An' nen he say
All wite, he'll show me there; an' tell me nen
To set him down wite easy on his feet,
An' loosen up the stwing a little where
It cut him under th' arms. An' nen he says,
"Come on!" he says; an' went a-limpin' 'long
The garden-paph—an' limpin' 'long an' 'long
Tel—purty soon he come on 'long to where's
A grea'-big cabbage-leaf. An' he stoop down
An' say, "Come on inunder here wiv me!"

50

So *I* stoop down an' crawl inunder there,
Like he say.

                An' inunder there's a grea'-
Big clod, they is—a' awful grea'-big clod!
An' nen he says, *"Woll this-here clod away!"*
An' so I woll' the clod away. An' nen
It's all wet, where the dew'z inunder where
The old clod wuz.—An' nen the Fairy he
Git on the wet-place: Nen he say to me,
"Git on the wet-place, too!" An' nen he say,
"Now hold yer breff an' shet yer eyes!" he says,
"Tel I say *Squinchy-winchy!"* Nen he say—
Somepin' *in Dutch,* I guess.—An' nen I felt
Like we 'uz sinkin' down—an' sinkin' down!—
Tel purty soon the little Fairy weach
An' pinch my nose an' yell at me an' say,
"Squinchy-winchy! Look wherever you please!"
Nen when I looked—Oh! they 'uz purtiest place
Down there you ever saw in all the World!—
They 'uz ist *flowers* an' *woses*—yes, an' *twees*
Wiv *blossoms* on an' *big wipe apples* boff!
An' butterflies, they wuz—an' hummin'-birds—
An' *yeller*birds an' *blue*birds—yes, an' *wed!*—
An' ever'wheres an' all awound 'uz vines
Wiv wipe p'serve-pears on 'em!—Yes, an' all
An' ever'thing 'at's ever growin' in

A garden—er canned up—all wipe at wunst!—
It wuz ist like a garden—only it
'Uz ist a *little bit* o' garden—'bout big wound
As ist our twun'el-bed is.—An' all wound
An' wound the little garden's a gold fence—
An' little gold gate, too—an' ash-hopper
'At's all gold, too—an' ist full o' gold ashes!
An' wite in th' middle o' the garden wuz
A little gold house, 'at's ist 'bout as big
As ist a bird-cage is: An' *in* the house
They 'uz whole-lots *more* Fairies there—'cause I
Picked up the little house, an' peeked in at
The winders, an' I see 'em all in there
Ist *buggin'* round! An' Mr. Squidjicum
He twy to make me quit, but I gwab *him*
An' poke him down the chimbly, too, I did!—
An' y'ort to see *him* hop out 'mongst 'em there!—
Ist like he 'uz the boss an' ist got back!—
"Hain't ye got on them-air dew-dumplin's yet?"
He says.

   An' they says no.

      An' nen he says—
"Better git at 'em nen!" he says, *"wite quick—
'Cause old Miss Hoodjicum's a-comin'!"*

        Nen
They all set wound a little gold tub—an'

All 'menced a-peelin' dewdwops, ist like they
'Uz *peaches*.—An', it looked so funny, I
Ist laugh' out loud, an' *dwopped* the little house,—
An' 't bu'sted like a soap-bubble!—an' 't skeered
Me so, I—I—I—I,—it skeered me so,—
I—ist *waked* up.—No! I *ain't* be'n *asleep*
An' *dweam* it all, like *you* think,—but it's shore
Fer-certain *fact* an' cwoss my heart it is!

THE MAN IN THE MOON

SAID The Raggedy Man, on a hot afternoon:
      My!
            Sakes!
                  What a lot o' mistakes
Some little folks makes on The Man in the Moon!
But people that's be'n up to *see* him, like *me*,
And calls on him frequent and intimuttly,
Might drop a few facts that would interest you
      Clean!
            Through!—
                  If you wanted 'em to—
Some *actual* facts that might interest you!

54

O The Man in the Moon has a crick in his back;
    Whee!
        Whimm!
            Ain't you sorry for him?
And a mole on his nose that is purple and black;
And his eyes are so weak that they water and run
If he dares to *dream* even he looks at the sun,—
So he jes dreams of stars, as the doctors advise—
    My!
        Eyes!
            But isn't he wise—
To jes dream of stars, as the doctors advise?

And The Man in the Moon has a boil on his ear—
    Whee!
        Whing!
            What a singular thing!
I know! but these facts are authentic, my dear,—
There's a boil on his ear; and a corn on his chin—
He calls it a dimple—but dimples stick in—
Yet it might be a dimple turned over, you know!
    Whang!
        Ho!
            Why, certainly so!—
It might be a dimple turned over, you know!

And The Man in the Moon has a rheumatic knee—
    Gee!
        Whizz!
            What a pity that is!
And his toes have worked round where his heels
    ought to be.—
So whenever he wants to go North he goes *South,*
And comes back with porridge-crumbs all round his
    mouth,
And he brushes them off with a Japanese fan,
    Whing!
        Whann!
            What a marvellous man!
What a very remarkably marvellous man!

'N' The Man in the Moon, sighed The Raggedy Man,
    Gits!
        So!
            Sullonesome, you know,—
Up there by hisse'f sence creation began!—
That when *I* call on him and then come away,
He grabs me and holds me and begs me to stay,—
Till—*Well!* if it wasn't fer *Jimmy-cum-jim,*
    Dadd!
        Limb!
            I'd go pardners with him—
Jes jump mv job here and be pardners with *him!*

O HEART of mine, we shouldn't
    Worry so!
What we've missed of calm we couldn't
    Have, you know!
What we've met of stormy pain,
And of sorrow's driving rain,
We can better meet again,
      If it blow!

We have erred in that dark hour
    We have known,
When our tears fell with the shower,
    All alone!—
Were not shine and shower blent
As the gracious Master meant?—
Let us temper our content
    With His own.

For, we know, not every morrow
    Can be sad;
So, forgetting all the sorrow
    We have had,
Let us fold away our fears,
And put by our foolish tears,
And through all the coming years
    Just be glad.

LET SOMETHING GOOD BE SAID

WHEN over the fair fame of friend or foe
    The shadow of disgrace shall fall, instead
    Of words of blame, or proof of thus and so,
Let something good be said.

Forget not that no fellow-being yet
    May fall so low but love may lift his head:
Even the cheek of shame with tears is wet,
    If something good be said.

No generous heart may vainly turn aside
    In ways of sympathy; no soul so dead
But may awaken strong and glorified,
    If something good be said.

And so I charge ye, by the thorny crown,
    •And by the cross on which the Saviour bled,
And by your own soul's hope of fair renown,
    Let something good be said!

THE FUNNIEST THING IN THE WORLD

THE funniest thing in the world, I know,
    Is watchin' the monkeys 'at's in the show!—
    Jumpin' an' runnin' an' racin' roun',
'Way up the top o' the pole; nen down!
First they're here, an' nen they're there,
An' ist a'most any an' ever'where!—
Screechin' an' scratchin' wherever they go,
They're the funniest thing in the world, I know!

They're the funniest thing in the world, I think:—
Funny to watch 'em eat an' drink;
Funny to watch 'em a-watchin' us,
An' actin' 'most like grown folks does!—
Funny to watch 'em p'tend to be
Skeerd at their tail 'at they happen to see;—
But the funniest thing in the world they do
Is never to laugh, like me an' you!

SOME SCATTERING REMARKS OF BUB'S

WUNST I tooked our pepper-box lid
An' cut little pie-dough biscuits, I did,
An' cooked 'em on our stove one day
When our hired girl she said I may.

Honey's the *goodest* thing—Oo-*ooh!*
An' blackburry-pies is goodest, too!
But wite hot biscuits, ist soakin' wet
Wiv tree-mullasus, is goodest yet!

Miss Maimie she's my Ma's friend,—an'
She's purtiest girl in all the lan'!—
An' sweetest smile an' voice an' face—
An' eyes ist looks like p'serves tas'e!

I *ruther* go to the Circus-show;
But, 'cause my *parunts* told me so,
I ruther go to the Sund'y School,
'Cause there I learn the goldun rule.

Say, Pa,—what *is* the goldun rule
'At's allus at the Sund'y School?

60

THE CIRCUS-DAY PARADE

OH, THE Circus-Day Parade! How the bugles
played and played!
And how the glossy horses tossed their flossy manes
and neighed,
As the rattle and the rhyme of the tenor-drummer's time
Filled all the hungry hearts of us with melody sublime!

How the grand band-wagon shone with a splender all
its own,
And glittered with a glory that our dreams had never
known!
And how the boys behind, high and low of every kind,
Marched in unconscious capture, with a rapture
undefined!

How the horsemen, two and two, with their plumes of
    white and blue,
And crimson, gold and purple, nodding by at me and
    you,
Waved the banners that they bore, as the Knights in days
    of yore,
Till our glad eyes gleamed and glistened like the spangles
    that they wore!

How the graceless-graceful stride of the elephant was
    eyed,
And the capers of the little horse that cantered at his side!
How the shambling camels, tame to the plaudits of their
    fame,
With listless eyes came silent, masticating as they came.

How the cages jolted past, with each wagon battened fast,
And the mystery within it only hinted of at last
From the little grated square in the rear, and nosing there
The snout of some strange animal that sniffed the outer
    air!

And, last of all, The Clown, making mirth for all the
    town,
With his lips curved ever upward and his eyebrows ever
    down,

And his chief attention paid to the little mule that played
A tattoo on the dashboard with his heels, in the Parade.

Oh! the Circus-Day Parade! How the bugles played and
      played!
And how the glossy horses tossed their flossy manes and
      neighed,
As the rattle and the rhyme of the tenor-drummer's time
Filled all the hungry hearts of us with melody sublime!

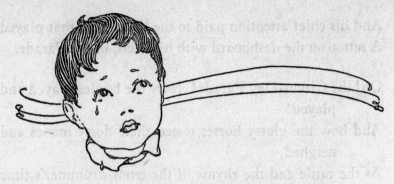

ALMOST BEYOND ENDURANCE

I AIN'T a-goin' to cry no more no more!
   I'm got ear-ache, an' Ma can't make
     It quit a-tall;
     An' Carlo bite my rubber-ball
   An' puncture it; an' Sis she take
An' poke' my knife down through the stable-floor
   An' loozed it—blame it all!
But I ain't goin' to cry no more no more!

An' Aunt Mame *wrote* she's comin', an' she *can't—*
   Folks is come *there!*—An' I don't care
     She *is* my Aunt!
     An' my eyes stings; an' I'm
     Ist coughin' all the time,
An' hurts me so, an' where my side's so sore
   Grampa felt where, an' he
   Says "Mayby it's *pleurasy!*"
But I ain't goin' to cry no more no more!

An' I clumbed up an' nen falled off the fence,
  An' Herbert he ist laugh at me!
    An' my fi'-cents
It sticked in my tin bank, an' I ist tore
  Purt'-nigh my thumbnail off, a-tryin' to git
  It out—nen *smash* it!—An' it's in there yit!
But I ain't goin' to cry no more no more!

Oo! I'm so wickud!—An' my breath's so *hot*—
  Ist like I run an' don't res' none
But ist run on when I ought to not;
    Yes, an' my chin
  An' lips 's all warpy, an' teeth's so fast,
  An' 's a place in my throat I can't swaller past—
    An' they all hurt so!—
    An' oh, my-oh!
    I'm a-startin' ag'in—
I'm a-*startin'* ag'in, but I *won't,* fer shore!—
I ist ain't goin' to cry no more no more!

LOCKERBIE STREET

SUCH a dear little street it is, nestled away
   From the noise of the city and heat of the day,
   In cool shady coverts of whispering trees,
With their leaves lifted up to shake hands with the
     breeze
Which in all its wide wanderings never may meet
With a resting-place fairer than Lockerbie Street!

There is such a relief, from the clangor and din
Of the heart of the town, to go loitering in
Through the dim, narrow walks, with the sheltering
     shade
Of the trees waving over the long promenade,
And littering lightly the ways of our feet
With the gold of the sunshine of Lockerbie Street.

And the nights that come down the dark pathways of
     dusk,
With the stars in their tresses, and odors of musk
In their moon-woven raiments, bespangled with dews,
And looped up with lilies for lovers to use
In the songs that they sing to the tinkle and beat
Of their sweet serenadings through Lockerbie Street.

O my Lockerbie Street! You are fair to be seen—
Be it noon of the day, or the rare and serene
Afternoon of the night—you are one to my heart,
And I love you above all the phrases of art,
For no language could frame and no lips could repeat
My rhyme-haunted raptures of Lockerbie Street.

HER LONESOMENESS

WHEN little Elizabeth whispers
    Her morning-love to me,
    Each word of the little lisper's,
As she clambers on my knee—
Hugs me and whispers, "Mommy,
  Oh, I'm so glad it's day
And the night's all gone away!"
How it does thrill and awe me,—
  "The night's all gone away!"

"Sometimes I wake, all listenin',"
  She sighs, "and all's so still!—
The moon and the stars half-glistenin'
  Over the window-sill;—
And I look where the gas's pale light
  Is all turned down in the hall—
And you ain't here at all!—
And oh, how I wish it was daylight!
  —And you ain't here at all!

"And oh," she goes eerily whining
  And laughing, too, as she speaks,
"If only the sun kept shining
  For weeks and weeks and weeks!—
For the world's so dark, without you,
  And the moon's turned down so low—
  'Way in the night, you know,—
And I get so lonesome about you!—
  'Way in the night, you know!"

THE RAGGEDY MAN ON CHILDREN

CHILDERN—take 'em as they run—
You kin *bet* on, ev'ry one!—
Treat 'em right and reco'nize
Human souls is all one size.

Jevver think?—the world's best men
Wears the same souls they had when
They run barefoot—'way back where
All these little childern air.

Heerd a boy, not long ago,
Say his parents *sassed* him so,
He'd *correct* 'em ef he could,—
Then be good ef *they'd* be good.

THE HIRED MAN'S FAITH IN CHILDREN

I BELIEVE *all* childern's good,
Ef they're only *understood*,—
Even *bad* ones 'pears to me
'S jes' as good as they kin be!

THE NINE LITTLE GOBLINS

THEY all climbed up on a high board-fence—
    Nine little goblins, with green-glass eyes—
    Nine little goblins that had no sense,
And couldn't tell coppers from cold mince-pies;
And they all climbed up on the fence, and sat—
And I asked them what they were staring at.

And the first one said, as he scratched his head
    With a queer little arm that reached out of his ear
And rasped its claws in his hair so red—
    "This is what this little arm is fer!"
      And he scratched and stared, and the next one said,
      "How on earth do *you* scratch your head?"

And he laughed like the screech of a rusty hinge—
   Laughed and laughed till his face grew black;
And when he choked, with a final twinge
   Of his stifling laughter, he thumped his back
      With a fist that grew on the end of his tail
      Till the breath came back to his lips so pale.

And the third little goblin leered round at me—
   And there were no lids on his eyes at all—
And he clucked one eye, and he says, says he,
   "What is the style of your socks this fall?"
      And he clapped his heels—and I sighed to see
      That he had hands where his feet should be.

Then a bald-faced goblin, gray and grim,
   Bowed his head, and I saw him slip
His eyebrows off, as I looked at him,
   And paste them over his upper lip;
      And then he moaned in remorseful pain—
      "Would—ah, would I'd me brows again!"

And then the whole of the goblin band
   Rocked on the fence-top to and fro,
And clung, in a long row, hand in hand,
   Singing the songs that they used to know—
      Singing the songs that their grandsires sung
      In the goo-goo days of the goblin-tongue.

And ever they kept their green-glass eyes
    Fixed on me with a stony stare—
Till my own grew glazed with a dread surmise,
    And my hat whooped up on my lifted hair,
        And I felt the heart in my breast snap to,
        As you've heard the lid of a snuff-box do.

And they sang: "You're asleep! There is no board-
        fence,
    And never a goblin with green-glass eyes!—
'Tis only a vision the mind invents
    After a supper of cold mince-pies,—
        And you're doomed to dream this way," they
            said,—
        *"And you shan't wake up till you're clean plum
            dead!"*

THE PIXY PEOPLE

IT was just a very
    Merry fairy dream!—
All the woods were airy
    With the gloom and gleam;
Crickets in the clover
    Clattered clear and strong,
And the bees droned over
    Their old honey-song.

In the mossy passes,
    Saucy grasshoppers
Leapt about the grasses
    And the thistle-burs;
And the whispered chuckle
    Of the katydid
Shook the honeysuckle
    Blossoms where he hid.

75

Through the breezy mazes
  Of the lazy June,
Drowsy with the hazes
  Of the dreamy noon,
Little Pixy people
  Winged above the walk,
Pouring from the steeple
  Of a mullein-stalk.

One—a gallant fellow—
  Evidently King,—
Wore a plume of yellow
  In a jewelled ring
On a pansy bonnet,
  Gold and white and blue,
With the dew still on it,
  And the fragrance, too.

One—a dainty lady—
  Evidently Queen,—
Wore a gown of shady
  Moonshine and green,
With a lace of gleaming
  Starlight that sent
All the dewdrops dreaming
  Everywhere she went.

One wore a waistcoat
  Of roseleaves, out and in,
And one wore a faced-coat
  Of tiger-lily-skin;
And one wore a neat coat
  Of palest galingale;
And one a tiny street-coat,
  And one a swallow-tail.

And Ho! sang the King of them
  And Hey! sang the Queen;
And round and round the ring of them
  Went dancing o'er the green;
And Hey! sang the Queen of them,
  And Ho! sang the King—
And all that I had seen of them
  —Wasn't anything!

It was just a very
  Merry fairy dream!—
All the woods were airy
  With the gloom and gleam;
Crickets in the clover
  Clattered clear and strong,
And the bees droned over
  Their old honey-song!

THE PRAYER PERFECT

DEAR Lord! kind Lord!
    Gracious Lord! I pray
    Thou wilt look on all I love,
    Tenderly to-day!
Weed their hearts of weariness;
    Scatter every care
Down a wake of angel-wings
    Winnowing the air.

Bring unto the sorrowing
    All release from pain;
Let the lips of laughter
    Overflow again;
And with all the needy
    O divide, I pray,
This vast treasure of content
    That is mine to-day!

REACH YOUR HAND TO ME

REACH your hand to me, my friend,
   With its heartiest caress—
   Sometime there will come an end
To its present faithfulness—
   Sometime I may ask in vain
   For the touch of it again,
   When between us land or sea
   Holds it ever back from me.

Sometime I may need it so,
   Groping somewhere in the night,
It will seem to me as though
   Just a touch, however light,
     Would make all the darkness day,
     And along some sunny way
     Lead me through an April-shower
     Of my tears to this fair hour.

O the present is too sweet
   To go on forever thus!
Round the corner of the street
   Who can say what waits for us?—
     Meeting—greeting, night and day,
     Faring each the selfsame way—
     Still somewhere the path must end—
     Reach your hand to me, my friend!

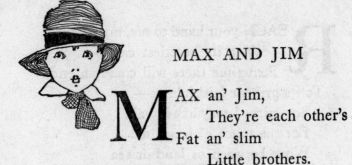

MAX AND JIM

MAX an' Jim,
    They're each other's
Fat an' slim
    Little brothers.

Max is thin,
    An' Jim, the fac's is,
Fat ag'in
    As little Max is!

Their Pa 'lowed
    He don't know whuther
He's most proud
    Of one er th'other!

Their Ma says
    They're both so sweet—'m!—
That she guess
    She'll haf to *eat* 'em!

THE SCHOOLBOY'S FAVORITE

*O*VER *the river and through the wood*
 Now Grandmother's cap I spy:
Hurrah for the fun!—Is the pudding done?
 Hurrah for the pumpkin pie!
—SCHOOL READER.

Fer any boy 'at's little as me,
 Er any little girl,
That-un's the goodest poetry piece
 In any book in the worl'!
An' ef grown-peoples wuz little ag'in
 I bet they'd say so, too,
Ef *they'd* go see *their* old Gran'ma,
 Like our Pa lets *us* do!

Over the river an' through the wood
  Now Gran'mother's cap I spy:
Hurrah fer the fun!—Is the puddin' done?—
  Hurrah fer the punkin-pie!

An' 'll tell *you* why 'at's the goodest piece:—
  'Cause it's ist like *we* go
To *our* Gran'ma's, a-visitun there,
  When our Pa he says so;
An' Ma she fixes my little cape-coat
  An' little fuzz-cap; an' Pa
He tucks me away—an' yells "Hoo-ray!"—
An' whacks Old Gray, an' drives the sleigh
  Fastest you ever saw!

Over the river an' through the wood
  Now Gran'mother's cap I spy:
Hurrah fer the fun!—Is the puddin' done?—
  Hurrah fer the punkin-pie!

An' Pa ist snuggles me 'tween his knees—
  An' I he'p hold the lines,
An' peek out over the buffalo-robe;—
An' the wind ist *blows!*—an' the snow ist *snows!*
  An' the sun ist shines! an' shines! —
An' th' ole horse tosses his head an' coughs
  The frost back in our face,—
An' I'd ruther go to my Gran'ma's
  Than any other place!

82

Over the river an' through the wood
  Now Gran'mother's cap I spy:
Hurrah fer the fun!—Is the puddin' done?—
  Hurrah fer the punkin-pie!

An' all the peoples they is in town
  Watches us whizzin' past
To go a-visitun our Gran'ma's,
  Like we all went there last;—
But *they* can't go, like ist *our* folks
  An' Johnny an' Lotty, and three
Er four neighber childerns, an' Rober-ut Volney,
  An' Charley an' Maggy an' me!

Over the river an' through the wood
  Now Gran'mother's cap I spy:
Hurrah fer the fun!—Is the puddin' done?—
  Hurrah fer the punkin-pie!

THE OLD TRAMP

A' OLD Tramp slep' in our stable wunst,
An' The Raggedy Man he caught
An' roust him up, an' chased him off
Clean out through our back lot!

An' th' old Tramp hollered back an' said,—
"You're a *purty* man!—*You* air!—
With a pair o' eyes like two fried eggs,
An' a nose like a Bartlutt pear!"

AN IMPETUOUS RESOLVE

WHEN little Dickie Swope's a man,
    He's go' to be a Sailor;
    An' little Hamey Tincher, he's
A-go' to be a Tailor:
Bud Mitchell, he's a-go' to be
    A stylish Carriage-Maker;
An' when *I* grow a grea'-big man,
    I'm go' to be a Baker!

An' Dick'll buy his sailor-suit
    O' Hame; an' Hame'll take it
An' buy as fine a double-rig
    As ever Bud kin make it:
An' nen all three'll drive roun' fer me,
    An' we'll drive off togevver,
A-slingin' pie-crust 'long the road
    Ferever an' ferever!

GRANNY

GRANNY'S come to our house,
　　And ho! my lawzy-daisy!
　　All the childern round the place
　Is ist a-runnin' crazy!
Fetched a cake fer little Jake,
　And fetched a pie fer Nanny,
And fetched a pear fer all the pack
　That runs to kiss their Granny!

Lucy Ellen's in her lap,
　And Wade and Silas-Walker
Both's a-ridin' on her foot,
　And Pollos on the rocker;
And Marthy's twins, from Aunt Marinn's,
　And little Orphant Annie,
All's a-eatin' gingerbread
　And giggle-un at Granny!

86

Tells us all the fairy tales
    Ever thought er wundered—
And 'bundance o' other stories—
    Bet she knows a hunderd!—
Bob's the one fer "Whittington,"
    And "Golden Locks" fer Fanny!
Hear 'em laugh and clap their hands,
    Listenun' at Granny!

"Jack the Giant-Killer" 's good;
    And "Bean-Stalk" 's another!—
So's the one of "Cinderell'"
    And her old godmother;—
That-un's best of all the rest—
    Bestest one of any,—
Where the mices scampers home,
    Like we runs to Granny!

Granny's come to our house,
    Ho! my lawzy-daisy!
All the childern round the place
    Is ist a-runnin' crazy!
Fetched a cake fer little Jake,
    And fetched a pie fer Nanny,
And fetched a pear fer all the pack
    That runs to kiss their Granny!

THE ORCHARD LANDS OF LONG AGO

THE orchard lands of Long Ago!
 O drowsy winds, awake, and blow
 The snowy blossoms back to me,
And all the buds that used to be!
Blow back along the grassy ways
Of truant feet, and lift the haze
Of happy summer from the trees
That trail their tresses in the seas
Of grain that float and overflow
The orchard lands of Long Ago!

Blow back the melody that slips
In lazy laughter from the lips
That marvel much if any kiss
Is sweeter than the apple's is.
Blow back the twitter of the birds—
The lisp, the titter, and the words
Of merriment that found the shine
Of summer-time a glorious wine
That drenched the leaves that loved it so,
In orchard lands of Long Ago!

O memory! alight and sing
Where rosy-bellied pippins cling,
And golden russets glint and gleam,
As, in the old Arabian dream,
The fruits of that enchanted tree
The glad Aladdin robbed for me!
And, drowsy winds, awake and fan
My blood as when it overran
A heart ripe as the apples grow
In orchard lands of Long Ago!

A BEAR FAMILY

WUNZT, 'way West in Illinoise,
    Wuz two Bears an' their two boys:
    An' the two boys' names, you know,
Wuz—like *ours* is,—Jim an' Jo;
An' their parunts' names wuz same's
All big grown-up people's names,—
Ist *Miz* Bear, the neighbers call
'Em, an' *Mister* Bear—'at's all.
Yes—an' Miz Bear scold him, too,
Ist like grown folks *shouldn't* do!
Wuz a grea'-big river there,
An', 'crosst that, 's a mountain where
Old Bear said some day he'd go,
Ef she don't quit scoldin' so!
So, one day when he been down
The river, fishin', 'most to town,

90

An' come back 'thout no fish a-tall,
An' Jim and Jo they run an' bawl
An' tell their ma their pa hain't fetch'
No fish,—she scold again an' ketch
Her old broom up an' biff him, too.—
An' he ist cry, an' say, "Boo-hoo!
I *told* you what I'd do some day!"
An' he ist turned an' runned away
To where's the grea'-big river there,
An' ist *splunged* in an' swum to where
The mountain's at, 'way th' other side,
An' clumbed up there. An' Miz Bear *cried*—
'An' little Jo an' little Jim—
Ist like their ma—bofe cried fer him!—
But he clumbed on, *clean out o' sight,*
He wuz so mad!—An' served 'em right!
Nen—when the Bear got 'way on top
The mountain, he heerd somepin' flop
Its wings—an' somepin' else he heerd
A-rattlin'-like.—An' he wuz *skeered,*
An' looked 'way up, an'—*Mercy sake!*
It wuz a' Eagul an' a *snake!*
An'-sir, the Snake, he bite an' kill'
The Eagul, an' they bofe fall till
They strike the ground—*k'spang-k'spat!*
Wite where the Bear wuz standin' at!
An' when here come the Snake at *him,*

The Bear he think o' little Jim
An' Jo, he did—an' their ma, too,—
All safe at home,—an' he ist flew
Back down the mountain—an' could hear
The old Snake rattlin', sharp an' clear,
Wite clos't behind!—An' Bear he's so
All tired out, by time, you know,
He git down to the river there,
He know' he can't *swim* back to where
His folks is at. But ist wite nen
He see a boat an' six big men
'At's been a-shootin' ducks: An' so
He skeered them out the boat, you know,
An' ist jumped in—an' Snake *he* tried
To jump in, too, but falled outside
Where all the water wuz; an' so
The Bear grabs one the things you row
The boat wiv an' ist whacks the head
Of the old Snake an' kills him dead!—
An' when he's killed him dead, w'y, nen
The old Snake's drownded dead again!
Nen Bear set in the boat an' bowed
His back an' rowed—an' rowed—an' rowed—
Till he's safe home—so tired he can't
Do nothin' but lay there an' pant
An' tell his childern, "Bresh my coat!"

An' tell his wife, "Go chain my boat!"
An' they're so glad he's back, they say
"They *knowed* he's comin' thataway
To ist su'prise the dear ones there!"
An' Jim an' Jo they dried his hair
An' pulled the burs out; an' their ma
She ist set there an' helt his paw
Till he wuz sound asleep, an' nen
She telled him she won't scold again—
Never—never—never—
Ferever an' ferever!

THE BUMBLEBEE

YOU better not fool with a Bumblebee!—
Ef you don't think they can sting—you'll see!
They're lazy to look at, an' kindo' go
Buzzin' an' bummin' aroun' so slow,
An' ac' so slouchy an' all fagged out,
Danglin' their legs as they drone about
The hollyhawks 'at they can't climb in
'Ithout ist a-tumble-un out ag'in!
Wunst I watched one climb clean 'way
In a jimpson-blossom, I did, one day,—
An' I ist *grabbed* it—an' nen let go—
An' *"Ooh-ooh! Honey! I told ye so!"*
Says the Raggedy Man; an' he ist run
An' pullt out the stinger, an' don't laugh none,
An' says: "They *has* be'n folks, I guess,
'At thought I wuz predjudust more er less,—
Yit I still muntain 'at a Bumblebee
Wears out his welcome too quick fer me!"

THE TOY PENNY-DOG

MA put my Penny-Dog
    Safe on the shelf,
    An' left no one home but him,
  Me an' myself;
So I clumbed a big chair
  I pushed to the wall—
But the Toy Penny-Dog
  Ain't there at all!
I went back to Dolly—
  An' *she* 'uz gone too,
An' little Switch 'uz layin' there;—
  An' Ma says *"Boo!"*—
An' there she wuz a-peepin'
  Through the front-room door:
An' I ain't goin' to be bad
  Little girl no more!

95

OUR BETSY

US childern 's all so lonesome
   We hardly want to *play*
Or skip or swing or anything,—
   'Cause Betsy she's away!
She's gone to see her people
   At her old home.—But then—
Oh! ev'ry child 'll jist be wild
   When she's back here again!

Then it's whoopty-doopty dooden!—
   Whoopty-dooden then!
Oh! it's whoopty-doopty dooden,
   When Betsy's back again!

She's like a mother to us,
   And like a sister, too—
Oh! she's as sweet as things to eat
   When all the dinner 's through!
And hey! to hear her laughin'!
   And ho! to hear her sing!—
To have her back is all we lack
   Of havin' *ev'rything!*

Then it's whoopty-doopty dooden!—
Whoopty-dooden then!
Oh! it's whoopty-doopty dooden,
When Betsy's back again!

Oh! some may sail the northern lakes,
    And some to foreign lands,
And some may seek old Nameless Creek,
    Or India's golden sands;
Or some may go to Kokomo,
    And some to Mackinac,—
But I'll go down to Morgantown
    To fetch our Betsy back.

Then it's whoopty-doopty dooden!—
Whoopty-dooden then!
Oh! it's whoopty-doopty dooden,
When Betsy's back again!

LULLABY

THE maple strews the embers of its leaves
    O'er the laggard swallows nestled 'neath the
       eaves
And the moody cricket falters in his cry—
      Baby-bye!—
And the lid of night is falling o'er the sky—
      Baby-bye!—
The lid of night is falling o'er the sky!

The rose is lying pallid, and the cup
Of the frosted calla-lily folded up;
And the breezes through the garden sob and sigh—
      Baby-bye!—
O'er the sleeping blooms of summer where they lie—
      Baby-bye!—
O'er the sleeping blooms of summer where they lie!

Yet, Baby—O my Baby, for your sake
This heart of mine is ever wide awake,
And my love may never droop a drowsy eye—
      Baby-bye!—
Till your own are wet above me when I die—
      Baby-bye!—
Till your own are wet above me when I die.

THE DAYS GONE BY

O THE days gone by! O the days gone by!
The apples in the orchard, and the pathway
through the rye;
The chirrup of the robin, and the whistle of the quail
As he piped across the meadows sweet as any night-
ingale;
When the bloom was on the clover, and the blue was in
the sky,
And my happy heart brimmed over, in the days gone by.

In the days gone by, when my naked feet were tripped
By the honeysuckle tangles where the water-lilies
dipped,
And the ripples of the river lipped the moss along the
brink
Where the placid-eyed and lazy-footed cattle came to
drink,
And the tilting snipe stood fearless of the truant's way-
ward cry
And the splashing of the swimmer, in the days gone by.

O the days gone by! O the days gone by!
The music of the laughing lip, the luster of the eye;
The childish faith in fairies, and Aladdin's magic ring—
The simple, soul-reposing, glad belief in every thing,—
When life was like a story holding neither sob nor sigh,
In the golden olden glory of the days gone by.

LITTLE COUSIN JASPER

LITTLE Cousin Jasper, he
　　Don't live in this town, like me,—
　　He lives 'way to Rensselaer,
An' ist comes to visit here.

He says 'at our court-house square
Ain't nigh big as theirn is there!—
He says their town's big as four
Er five towns like this, an' more!

He says ef his folks moved here
He'd cry to leave Rensselaer—
'Cause they's prairie there, an' lakes,
An' wile-ducks an' rattlesnakes!

Yes, 'n' little Jasper's Pa
Shoots most things you ever saw!—
Wunst he shot a deer, one day,
'At swummed off an' got away.

Little Cousin Jasper went
An' camped out wunst in a tent
Wiv his Pa, an' helt his gun
While he kilt a turrapun.

An' when his Ma heerd o' that,
An' more things his Pa's bin at,
She says, "Yes, 'n' he'll git shot
'Fore he's man-grown, like as not!"

An' they's mussrats there, an' minks,
An' di-dippers, an' chee-winks,—
Yes, 'n' cal'mus-root you chew
All up an' 't 'on't pizen you!

An', in town, 's a flag-pole there—
Highest one 'at's anywhere
In this world!—wite in the street
Where the big mass-meetin's meet.

Yes, 'n' Jasper he says they
Got a brass band there, an' play
On it, an' march up an' down
An' all over round the town!

Wisht our town ain't like it is!—
Wisht it's ist as big as his!
Wisht 'at *his* folks they'd move *here,*
An' *we'd* move to Rensselaer!

IRY AND BILLY AND JO

A TINTYPE

IRY an' Billy an' Jo!—
   Iry an' Billy's *the boys,*
   An' *Jo's* their *dog,* you know,—
Their pictur's took all in a row.
   Bet they kin kick up a noise—
   Iry an' Billy, the boys,
An' that-air little dog Jo!

Iry's the one 'at stands
   Up there a-lookin' so mild
An' meek—with his hat in his hands,
   Like such a *'bediant* child—
(*Sakes-alive!*) —An' *Billy* he sets
In the cheer an' holds on to Jo an' *sweats*
Hisse'f, a-lookin' so good! Ho-ho!
   Iry an' Billy an' Jo!

Yit the way them boys, you know,
    Usen to jes' turn in
An' fight over that dog Jo
    Wuz a burnin'-shame-an'-a-sin!—
Iry *he'd* argy 'at, by gee-whizz!
That-air little Jo-dog wuz *his!*—
An' Billy *he'd* claim it wuzn't so—
'Cause the dog wuz *hisn!*—An' at it they'd go,
Nip-an'-tugg, tooth-an'-toe-nail, you know—
    Iry an' Billy an' Jo!

But their Pa—(He wuz the marshal then)—
    He 'tended-like 'at he *jerked 'em up;*
An' got a jury o' Brick-yard men
    An' helt a *trial* about the pup:
An' *he* says *he* jes' like to 'a' died
When the rest o' us town-boys *testified*—
    Regardin', you know,
    Iry an' Billy an' Jo!

'Cause we all knowed, when *the Gipsies* they
    Camped down here by the crick last Fall,
They brung Jo with 'em, an' give him away
    To Iry an' Billy fer nothin' at all!—
So the jury fetched in the *verdick* so
    Jo he ain't *neether* o' theirn fer *shore*—
    He's *both* their dog, an' jes' no more!
    An' so
    They've quit quarrelin' long ago,
    Iry an' Billy an' Jo.

THE RUNAWAY BOY

WUNST I sassed my Pa, an' he
Won't stand that, an' punished me,—
Nen when he was gone that day,
I slipped out an' runned away.

I tooked all my copper-cents,
An' clumbed over our back fence
In the jimpson-weeds 'at growed
Ever'where all down the road.

Nen I got out there, an' nen
I runned some—an' runned again
When I met a man 'at led
A big cow 'at shooked her head.

I went down a long, long lane
Where was little pigs a-play'n';
An' a grea'-big pig went "Booh!"
An' jumped up, an' skeered me too.

Nen I scampered past, an' they
Was somebody hollered "Hey!"
An' I ist looked ever'where,
An' they was nobody there.

I *want* to, but I'm 'fraid to try
To go back. . . .An' by-an'-by,
Somepin' hurts my throat inside—
An' I want my Ma—an' cried.

Nen' a grea'-big girl come through
Where's a gate, an' telled me who
Am I? an' ef I tell where
My home's at she'll show me there.

But I couldn't ist but tell
What's my *name;* an' she says well,
An' she tooked me up an' says
She know where I live, she guess.

Nen she telled me hug wite close
Round her neck!—an' off she goes
Skippin' up the street! An' nen
Purty soon I'm home again.

An' my Ma, when she kissed me,
Kissed the *big girl* too, an' *she*
Kissed me—ef I p'omise *shore*
I won't run away no more!

BILLY MILLER'S CIRCUS-SHOW

AT Billy Miller's Circus-Show—
      In their old stable where it's at—
      The boys pays twenty pins to go,
An' gits their money's-worth at that!—
'Cause Billy he can climb an' chalk
His stockin'-feet an' purt'-nigh walk
A tight-rope—yes, an' ef he fall
He'll ketch, an' "skin a cat"—'at's all!

He ain't afeard to swing an' hang
    Ist by his legs!—an' mayby stop
An' yell "Look out!" an' nen—k-spang!—
    He'll let loose, upside-down, an' drop
Wite on his hands! An' nen he'll do
"Contortion-acts"—ist limber through
As "Injarubber Mens" 'at goes
With shore-fer-certain circus-shows!

At Billy Miller's Circus-Show
   He's got a circus-ring—an' they's
A dressin'-room,—so's he can go
   An' dress an' paint up when he plays
He's somepin' else;—'cause sometimes he's
"Ringmaster"—bossin' like he please—
An' sometimes "Ephalunt"—er "Bare-
Back Rider," prancin' out o' there!

An' sometimes—an' the best of all!—
   He's "The Old Clown," an' got on clo'es
All stripud,—an' white hat, all tall
   An' peakud—like in shore-'nuff shows,—
An' got three-cornered red-marks, too,
On his white cheeks—ist like they do!—
An' you'd ist die, the way he sings
An' dances an' says funny things!

THE LAND OF USED-TO-BE

AND where's the Land of Used-to-be, does little
  baby wonder?
Oh, we will clap a magic saddle over "Pop-
  um's" knee
And ride away around the world, and in and out
  and under
The whole of all the golden sunny Summertime
  and see.

Leisurely and lazy-like we'll jostle on our journey,
  And let the pony bathe his hooves and cool them
    in the dew,
As he sidles down the shady way and lags along the
  ferny
  And green grassy edges of the lane we travel
    through.

And then we'll canter on to catch the bubble of the
    thistle
  As it bumps among the butterflies and glimmers
    down the sun,
To leave us laughing, all content to hear the robin
    whistle
  Or guess what Katydid is saying little Katy's done.

And pausing here a minute, where we hear the
    squirrel chuckie
  As he darts from out the underbrush and scampers
    up the tree,
We will gather buds and locust-blossoms, leaves and
    honeysuckle,
  To wreathe around our foreheads, riding into
    Used-to-be;—

For here's the very rim of it that we go swinging
    over—
  Don't you hear the Fairy bugles, and the tinkle of
    the bells,
And see the baby-bumblebees that tumble in the
    clover
  And dangle from the tilted pinks and tipsy pim-
    perneïs?

'And don't you see the merry faces of the daffodillies,
  And the jolly Johnny-jump-ups, and the buttercups
    a-glee,
And the low, lolling ripples ring around the water-
    lilies?—
  All greeting us with laughter, to the Land of
    Used-to-be!

And here among the blossoms of the blooming vines
    and grasses,
  With a haze forever hanging in a sky forever
    blue,
And with a breeze from over-seas to kiss us as it
    passes,
  We will romp around forever as the airy Elfins do!

For all the elves of earth and air are swarming here
    together—
  The prankish Puck, King Oberon, and Queen
    Titania too;
And dear old Mother Goose herself, as sunny as the
    weather,
  Comes dancing down the dewy walks to welcome
    me and you!

THE CLOVER

SOME sings of the lilly, and daisy, and rose,
   And the pansies and pinks that the Summer-
      time throws
In the green grassy lap of the medder that lays
Blinkin' up at the skyes through the sunshiny days;
But what is the lilly and all of the rest
Of the flowers, to a man with a hart in his brest
That was dipped brimmin' full of the honey and dew
Of the sweet clover-blossoms his babyhood knew?

I never set eyes on a clover-field now,
Er fool round a stable, er climb in the mow,
But my childhood comes back jest as clear and as plane
As the smell of the clover I'm sniffin' again;
And I wunder away in a barefooted dream,
Whare I tangle my toes in the blossoms that gleam
With the dew of the dawn of the morning of love
Ere it wept ore the graves that I'm weepin' above.

And so I love clover—it seems like a part
Of the sacerdest sorrows and joys of my hart;
And wherever it blossoms, oh, thare let me bow
And thank the good God as I'm thankin' Him now;
And I pray to Him still fer the stren'th when I die,
To go out in the clover and tell it good-by,
And lovin'ly nestle my face in its bloom
While my soul slips away on a breth of purfume.

OUT TO OLD AUNT MARY'S

WASN'T it pleasant, O brother mine,
In those old days of the lost sunshine
   Of youth—When the Saturday's chores
      were through,
      And the "Sunday's wood" in the
         kitchen, too,
      And we went visiting, "me and you,"
         Out to Old Aunt Mary's?—

"Me and you"—And the morning fair,
With the dewdrops twinkling everywhere;
   The scent of the cherry-blossoms blown
   After us, in the roadway lone,
   Our capering shadows onward thrown—
      Out to Old Aunt Mary's.

It all comes back so clear to-day!
Though I am as bald as you are gray,—
Out by the barn-lot and down the lane
We patter along in the dust again,
As light as the tips of the drops of the rain,
Out to Old Aunt Mary's.

The last few houses of the town;
Then on, up the high creek-bluffs and down;
Past the squat toll-gate, with its well-sweep pole;
The Bridge, and "the old 'babtizin'-hole,'"
Loitering, awed, o'er pool and shoal,
Out to Old Aunt Mary's.

We cross the pasture, and through the wood,
Where the old gray snag of the poplar stood,
Where the hammering "red-heads" hopped awry,
And the buzzard "raised" in the "clearing"-sky
And lolled and circled, as we went by
Out to Old Aunt Mary's.

Or, stayed by the glint of the redbird's wings,
Or the glitter of song that the bluebird sings,
All hushed we feign to strike strange trails,
As the "big braves" do in the Indian tales,
Till again our real quest lags and fails—
Out to Old Aunt Mary's.—

And the woodland echoes with yells of mirth
That make old war-whoops of minor worth! . . .
 Where such heroes of war as we?—
 With bows and arrows of fantasy,
 Chasing each other from tree to tree
  Out to Old Aunt Mary's!

And then in the dust of the road again;
And the teams we met, and the countrymen;
 And the long highway, with sunshine spread
 As thick as butter on country bread,
 Our cares behind, and our hearts ahead
  Out to Old Aunt Mary's.—

For only, now, at the road's next bend
To the right we could make out the gable-end
 Of the fine old Huston homestead—not
 Half a mile from the sacred spot
 Where dwelt our Saint in her simple cot—
  Out to Old Aunt Mary's.

Why, I see her now in the open door
Where the little gourds grew up the sides and o'er
 The clapboard roof!—And her face—ah, me!
 Wasn't it good for a boy to see—
 And wasn't it good for a boy to be
  Out to Old Aunt Mary's?—

The jelly—the jam and the marmalade,
And the cherry and quince "preserves" she made!
  And the sweet-sour pickles of peach and pear,
  With cinnamon in 'em and all things rare!—
  And the more we ate was the more to spare,
      Out to Old Aunt Mary's!

Ah, was there, ever, so kind a face
And gentle as hers, or such a grace
  Of welcoming, as she cut the cake
  Or the juicy pies that she joyed to make
  Just for the visiting children's sake—
      Out to Old Aunt Mary's!

The honey, too, in its amber comb
One only finds in an old farm-home;
  And the coffee, fragrant and sweet, and ho!
  So hot that we gloried to drink it so,
  With spangles of tears in our eyes, you know—
      Out to Old Aunt Mary's.

And the romps we took, in our glad unrest!—
Was it the lawn that we loved the best,
  With its swooping swing in the locust trees,
  Or was it the grove, with its leafy breeze,
  Or the dim haymow, with its fragrancies—
      Out to Old Aunt Mary's.

Far fields, bottom-lands, creek-banks—all,
We ranged at will.—Where the waterfall
　　Laughed all day as it slowly poured
　　Over the dam by the old mill-ford,
　　While the tail-race writhed, and the mill-wheel
　　　roared—
　　　　Out to Old Aunt Mary's.

But home, with Aunty in nearer call,
That was the best place, after all!—
　　The talks on the back porch, in the low
　　Slanting sun and the evening glow,
　　With the voice of counsel that touched us so,
　　　　Out to Old Aunt Mary's.

And then, in the garden—near the side
Where the beehives were and the path was wide,—
　　The apple-house—like a fairy cell—
　　With the little square door we knew so well,
　　And the wealth inside but our tongues could tell—
　　　　Out to Old Aunt Mary's.

And the old spring-house, in the cool green gloom
Of the willow trees,—and the cooler room
　　Where the swinging shelves and the crocks were
　　　kept,
　　Where the cream in a golden languor slept,
　　While the waters gurgled and laughed and wept—
　　　　Out to Old Aunt Mary's.

And as many a time have you and I—
Barefoot boys in the days gone by—
    Knelt, and in tremulous ecstasies
    Dipped our lips into sweets like these,—
    Memory now is on her knees
            Out to Old Aunt Mary's.—

For, O my brother so far away,
This is to tell you—she waits *to-day*
    To welcome us:—Aunt Mary fell
    Asleep this morning, whispering, "Tell
    The boys to come." . . . And all is well
            Out to Old Aunt Mary's.

THE OLD HAY-MOW

THE Old Hay-mow's the place to play
    Fer boys, when it's a rainy day!
    I good 'eal ruther be up there
Than down in town, er anywhere!

When I play in our stable-loft,
The good old hay's so dry an' soft,
An' feels so fine, an' smells so sweet,
I 'most ferget to go an' eat.

An' one time wunst I *did* ferget
To go 'tel dinner was all et,—
An' they had short-cake—an'—Bud he
Hogged up the piece Ma saved fer me.

121

Nen I won't let him play no more
In our hay-mow where I keep store
An' got hen-eggs to sell,—an' shoo
The cackle-un old hen out, too!

An' nen, when Aunty she was here
A-visitun from Rensselaer,
An' bringed my little cousin,—*He*
Can come up there an' play with me.

But, after while—when Bud he bets
'At I can't turn no summersetts,—
I let him come up, ef he can
Ac' ha'f-way like a gentleman!

THE SQUIRT-GUN UNCLE MAKED ME

UNCLE SIDNEY, when he wuz here,
 Maked me a squirt-gun out o' some
 Elder-bushes 'at growed out near
Where wuz the brick-yard—'way out clear
 To where the Toll Gate come!

So when we walked back home again,
 He maked it, out in our woodhouse where
Wuz the old work-bench, an' the old jack-plane,
An' the old 'poke-shave, an' the tools all lay'n'
 Ist like he wants 'em there.

123

He sawed it first with the old hand-saw;
  An' nen he peeled off the bark, an' got
Some glass an' scraped it; an' told 'bout **Pa**,
When *he* wuz a boy an' fooled his **Ma**,
  An' the whippin' 'at he caught.

Nen Uncle Sidney, he took an' filed
  A' old arn ramrod; an' one o' the ends
He screwed fast into the vise; an' smiled,
Thinkin', he said, o' when he wuz a child,
  'Fore him an' **Pa** wuz mens.

He punched out the peth, an' nen he putt
  A plug in the end with a hole notched through;
Nen took the old drawey-knife an' cut
An' maked a handle 'at shoved clean shut
  But ist where yer hand held to.

An' he wropt th' uther end with some string an' white
  Piece o' the sleeve of a' old tored shirt;
An' nen he showed me to hold it tight,
An' suck in the water an' work it right—
  An' it 'ud ist squirt an' squirt!

THE BOYS' CANDIDATE

L AS' time 'at Uncle Sidney come,
He bringed a watermelon home—
An' half the boys in town
Come taggin' after him.—An' he
Says, when we et it,—*"Gracious me!
'S the boy-house fell down?"*

LITTLE ORPHANT ANNIE

LITTLE Orphant Annie's come to our house to
      stay,
  An' wash the cups an' saucers up, an' bresh
      the crumbs away,
An' shoo the chickens off the porch, an' dust the
      hearth, an' sweep,
An' make the fire, an' bake the bread, an' earn her
      board-an'-keep;
An' all us other childern, when the supper-things is
      done,
We set around the kitchen fire an' has the mostest fun
A-list'nin' to the witch-tales 'at Annie tells about,
An' the Gobble-uns 'at gits you
          Ef you
            Don't
              Watch
                Out!

Onc't they was a little boy wouldn't say his prayers,—
So when he went to bed at night, away up stairs,
His Mammy heerd him holler, an' his Daddy heerd
      him bawl,
An' when they turn't the kivvers down, he wasn't
      there at all!
An' they seeked him in the rafter-room, an' cubby-
      hole, an' press,
An' seeked him up the chimbly-flue, an' ever'wheres,
      I guess;
But all they ever found was thist his pants an' round-
      about:—
An' the Gobble-uns'll git you
          Ef you
        Don't
      Watch
      Out!

An' one time a little girl 'ud allus laugh an' grin,
An' make fun of ever'one, an' all her blood an' kin;
An' onc't, when they was "company," an' ole folks
      was there,
She mocked 'em an' shocked 'em, an' said she didn't
      care!
An' thist as she kicked her heels, an' turn't to run an'
      hide,
They was two great big Black Things a-standin' by
      her side,

An' they snatched her through the ceilin' 'fore she
knowed what she's about!
An' the Gobble-uns'll git you
Ef you
Don't
Watch
Out!

An' little Orphant Annie says when the blaze is blue,
An' the lamp-wick sputters, an' the wind goes *woo-oo!*
An' you hear the crickets quit, an' the moon is gray,
An' the lightnin'-bugs in dew is all squenched away,—
You better mind yer parunts an' yer teachers fond
an' dear,
An' churish them 'at loves you, an' dry the orphant's
tear,
An' he'p the pore an' needy ones 'at clusters all about,
Er the Gobble-uns'll git you
Ef you
Don't
Watch
Out!

A SONG OF LONG AGO

A SONG of Long Ago:
　　Sing it lightly—sing it low—
　　Sing it softly—like the lisping of the lips we
　　　　we used to know
When our baby-laughter spilled
From the glad hearts ever filled
With music blithe as robin ever trilled!

Let the fragrant summer breeze,
And the leaves of locust-trees,
And the apple-buds and -blossoms, and the wings of
　　　　honey-bees,
All palpitate with glee,
Till the happy harmony
Brings back each childish joy to you and me.

Let the eyes of fancy turn
Where the tumbled pippins burn
Like embers in the orchard's lap of tangled grass and
　　　　fern,—
There let the old path wind
In and out, and on behind
The cider-press that chuckles as we grind.

Blend in the song the moan
Of the dove that grieves alone,
And the wild whir of the locust, and the bumble's
     drowsy drone;
And the low of cows that call
Through the pasture-bars when all
The landscape fades away at evenfall.

Then, far away and clear,
Through the dusky atmosphere,
Let the wailing of the killdee be the only sound we hear:
O sad and sweet and low
As the memory may know
Is the glad-pathetic song of Long Ago!

BILLY AND HIS DRUM

HO! it's come, kids, come!
With a bim! bam! bum!
Here's little Billy bangin' on
    his big bass drum!
He's a-marchin' round the room,
With his feather-duster plume
A-noddin' an' a-bobbin' with his
    bim! bam! boom!

Looky, little Jane an' Jim!
Will you only look at him,
A-humpin' an' a-thumpin' with his
    bam! bom! bim!
Has the Day o' Judgment come
Er the New Mi-len-nee-um?
Er is it only Billy with his
    bim! bam! bum!

I'm a-comin'; yes, I am—
Jim an' Sis, an' Jane an' Sam!
We'll all march off with Billy and his
    bom! bim! bam!
Come hur*raw*in' as you come,
Er they'll think you're deef-an'-dumb
Ef you don't hear little Billy an' his
    big bass drum!

THE BOY LIVES ON OUR FARM

THE Boy lives on our Farm, he's not
    Afeard o' horses none!
    An' he can make 'em lope, er trot,
Er rack, er pace, er run.
Sometimes he drives two horses, when
    He comes to town an' brings
A wagon-full o' 'taters nen,
    An' roastin'-ears an' things.

Two horses is "a team," he says,—
    An' when you drive er hitch,
The right-un's a "near-horse," I guess,
    Er "off"—I don't know which.—
The Boy lives on our Farm, he told
    Me, too, 'at he can see,
By lookin' at their teeth, how old
    A horse is, to a T!

I'd be the gladdest boy alive
   Ef I knowed much as that,
An' could stand up like him an' drive,
   An' ist push back my hat,
Like he comes skallyhootin' through
   Our alley, with one arm
A-wavin' Fare-ye-well! to you—
   The Boy lives on our Farm!

GOIN' TO THE FAIR
Old Style

WHEN Me an' my Ma an' Pa went to the Fair,
Ma borried Mizz Rollins-uz rigg to go there,
'Cause *our* buggy's *new,* an' Ma says, "Mercy-
sake!
It wouldn't hold *half* the folks *she's* go' to take!"
An' she took Marindy, an' Jane's twins, an' Jo,
An' Aunty Van Meters-uz girls—an' old Slo'
Magee, 'at's so fat, come a-scrougin' in there,
When me an' my Ma an' Pa went to the Fair!

The road's full o' loads-full 'ist ready to bu'st,
An' all hot, an' smokin' an' chokin' with dust;
The Wolffs an' their wagon, an' Brizentines, too—
An' horses 'ist r'ared when the toot-cars come through!
An' 'way from fur off we could hear the band play,
An' peoples all there 'u'd 'ist whoop an' hooray!
An' I stood on the dashboard, an' Pa boost' me there
'Most high as the fence, when we went to the Fair.

An' when we 'uz there an' inside, we could see
Wher' the flag's on a pole wher' a show's go' to be;
An' boys up in trees, an' the grea'-big balloon
'At didn't goned up a-tall, all afternoon!
An' a man in the crowd there gived money away—
An' Pa says *"he'd* ruther earn *his* by the day!"—
An' *he* gim-me some, an' says "ain't nothin' there
Too good fer his boy," when we went to the Fair.

Wisht the Raggedy Man wuz there, too!—but he says,
"Don't talk fairs to *me,* child! I went to one;—yes,—
An' there wuz a swing there ye rode—an' I rode,
An' a thing-um-a-jing 'at ye blowed—an' I blowed;
An' they wuz a game 'at ye played—an' I played,
An' a hitch in the same wher' ye paid—an' I paid;
An' they wuz *two* bad to one good peoples there—
Like *you* an' your *Pa* an' Ma went to the Fair!"

THE DOODLE BUGS'S CHARM

WHEN Uncle Sidney he comes here—
An' Fred an' me an' Min,—
My Ma she says she bet you yet
The roof'll tumble in!
For Uncle he ist *romps* with us:
An' wunst, out in our shed,
He told us 'bout the Doodle-Bugs,
An' what they'll do, he said,
Ef you'll ist holler "Doodle-Bugs!"—
Out by our garden-bed—
"Doodle-Bugs! Doodle-Bugs!
Come up an' git some bread!"

Ain't Uncle Sidney funny man?—
  "He's childish 'most as me"—
My Ma sometimes she tells him that—
  "He ac's so foolishly!"
W'y, wunst, out in our garden-path
  Wite by the pie-plant bed,
He all sprawled out there in the dirt
  An' ist scrooched down his head,
An' "Doodle! Doodle! Doodle-Bugs!"
  My Uncle Sidney said,—
"Doodle-Bugs! Doodle-Bugs!
  Come up an' git some bread!"

An' nen he showed us little holes
  All bored there in the ground,
An' little weenty heaps o' dust
  'At's piled there all around:
An' Uncle said, when he's like us,
  Er purt' nigh big as Fred,
That wuz the Doodle-Bugs's Charm—
  To call 'em up, he said:—
"Doodle! Doodle! Doodle-Bugs!"
  An' they'd poke out their head—
"Doodle-Bugs! Doodle-Bugs!
  Come up an' git some bread!"

MISTER HOP-TOAD

HOWDY, Mister Hop-Toad! Glad to see you out!
Bin a month o' Sund'ys sense I seen you here-
about.
Kind o' bin a-layin' in, from the frost and snow?
Good to see you out ag'in, it's bin so long ago!
Plow's like slicin' cheese, and sod's loppin' over even;
Loam's like gingerbread, and clod's softer'n deceivin'—
Mister Hop-Toad, honest-true—Spring-time—don't you
love it?
You old rusty rascal you, at the bottom of it!

Oh! oh! oh!
I grabs up my old hoe;
But I sees *you,*
And s' I, "Ooh-ooh!
Howdy, Mister Hop-Toad! How-dee-do!"

Make yourse'f more comfo'bler—square 'round at your
    ease—
Don't set saggin' slanchwise, with your nose below your
    knees.
Swell that fat old throat o' yourn and lemme see you
    swaller;
Straighten up and h'ist your head!—*You* don't owe a
    dollar!—
Hain't no mor'gage on your land—ner no taxes, nuther;
You don't haf to work no roads, even ef you'd ruther.
'F I was you, and *fixed* like you, I really wouldn't keer
To swap fer life and hop right in the presidential cheer!

> Oh! oh! oh!
> I hauls back my old hoe;
> But I sees *you,*
> And s' I, "Ooh-ooh!
> Howdy, Mister Hop-Toad! How-dee-do!"

'Long about next Aprile, hoppin' down the furry,
Won't you mind I ast you what 'peared to be the hurry?—
Won't you mind I hooked my hoe and hauled you back
    and smiled?—
W'y, bless you, Mister Hop-Toad, I love you like a child!
S'pose I'd want to 'flict you any more'n what you air?—
S'pose I think you got no rights 'cept the warts you wear?

Hulk, sulk, and blink away, you old bloat-eyed rowdy!—
Hain't you got a word to say?—Won't you tell me
"Howdy"?

Oh! oh! oh!
I swish round my old hoe;
But I sees *you,*
And s' I, "Ooh-ooh!
Howdy, Mister Hop-Toad! How-dee-do!"

OUR HIRED GIRL

OUR hired girl, she's 'Lizabuth Ann;
    An' she can cook best things to eat!
    She ist puts dough in our pie-pan,
An' pours in somepin' 'at's good and sweet,
An' nen she salts it all on top
With cinnamon; an' nen she'll stop
    An' stoop an' slide it, ist as slow,
In th' old cook-stove, so's 'twon't slop
    An' git all spilled; nen bakes it, so
    It's custard pie, first thing you know!
        An' nen she'll say:
    "Clear out o' my way!
    They's time fer work, an' time fer play!—
        Take yer dough, an' run, Child; run!
        Er I cain't git no cookin' done!"

When our hired girl 'tends like she's mad,
  An' says folks got to walk the chalk
When *she's* around, er wisht they had,
  I play out on our porch an' talk
To th' Raggedy Man 'at mows our lawn;
An' he says *"Whew!"* an' nen leans on
  His old crook-scythe, and blinks his eyes
An' sniffs all round an' says,—"I swawn!
  Ef my old nose don't tell me lies,
  It 'pears like I smell custard-pies!"
    An' nen *he'll* say,—
  "'Clear out o' my way!
  They's time fer work an' time fer play!
    Take yer dough, an' run, Child; run!
    Er *she* cain't git no cookin' done!'"

Wunst our hired girl, when she
  Got the supper, an' we all et,
An' it was night, an' Ma an' me
  An' Pa went wher' the "Social" met,—
An' nen when we come home, an' see
A light in the kitchen-door, an' we
  Heerd a maccordeun, Pa says "Lan'-
O'-Gracious! who can *her* beau be?"

An' I marched in, an' 'Lizabuth Ann
Wuz parchin' corn fer the Raggedy Man!
   Better say
"Clear out o' the way!
They's time fer work, an' time fer play!
   Take the hint, an' run, Child; run!
   Er we cain't git no *courtin'* done!"

WHEN EARLY MARCH SEEMS MIDDLE MAY

WHEN country roads begin to thaw
    In mottled spots of damp and dust,
   'And fences by the margin draw
  Along the frosty crust
Their graphic silhouettes, I say,
The Spring is coming round this way.

When morning-time is bright with sun
   And keen with wind, and both confuse
The dancing, glancing eyes of one
   With tears that ooze and ooze—
And nose-tips weep as well as they,
The Spring is coming round this way.

When suddenly some shadow-bird
   Goes wavering beneath the gaze,
And through the hedge the moan is heard
   Of kine that fain would graze
In grasses new, I smile and say,
The Spring is coming round this way.

When knotted horse-tails are untied,
   And teamsters whistle here and there,
And clumsy mitts are laid aside
   And choppers' hands are bare,

And chips are thick where children play,
The Spring is coming round this way.

When through the twigs the farmer tramps,
  And troughs are chunked beneath the trees,
And fragrant hints of sugar-camps
  Astray in every breeze,—
When early March seems middle May,
The Spring is coming round this way.

When coughs are changed to laughs, and when
  Our frowns melt into smiles of glee,
And all our blood thaws out again
  In streams of ecstasy,
And poets wreak their roundelay,
The Spring is coming round this way.

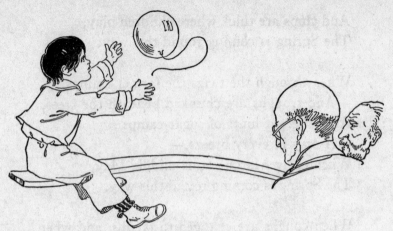

THE TOY-BALLOON

THEY wuz a Big Day wunst in town,
　　An' little Jason's Pa
　　Buyed him a little toy-balloon,
The first he ever saw.—
An' oh! but Jase wuz *more'n* proud,
　　A-holdin' to the string
An' scrougin' through the grea'-big crowd,
　　To hear the Glee Club sing.

The Glee Club it wuz goin' to sing
　　In old Masonic Hall;
An' Speakin', it wuz in there, too,
　　An' soldiers, folks an' all,
An' Jason's Pa he git a seat
　　An' set down purty soon,
A-holdin' little Jase, an' him
　　A-holdin' his balloon.

An' while the Speakin' 's startin' up
    An' ever'body still—
The first you know wuz little Jase
    A-yellin' fit to kill!—
Nen Jason's Pa jump on his seat
    An' grab up in the air,—
But little Jason's toy-balloon
    Wuz clean away from there!

An' Jase he yelled; an' Jase's Pa,
    Still lookin' up, clumb down—
While that-air little toy-balloon
    Went bumpin' roun' an' roun'
Ag'inst the ceilin', 'way up there
    Where ever'body saw,
An' *they* all yelled, an' *Jason* yelled
    An' little Jason's Pa!

But when his Pa he packed him out
    A-screamin'—nen the crowd
Looked down an' hushed—till they looked up
    An' howled ag'in out loud;
An' nen the speaker, mad an' pale,
    Jist turned an' left the stand,
An' all j'ined in the Glee Club—"Hail,
    Columby, Happy Land!"

THE BOY PATRIOT

I WANT to be a Soldier!—
                    A Soldier!—
                              A Soldier!—
I want to be a Soldier, with a saber in my hand
Or a little carbine rifle, or a musket on my shoulder,
Or just a snare-drum, snarling in the middle of the band;
I want to hear, high overhead, The Old Flag flap her
      wings
While all the Army, following, in chorus cheers and
      sings;
            I want to hear the tramp and jar
                  Of patriots a million,
            As gaily dancing off to war
                  As dancing a cotillion.

I want to be a Soldier!—
                    A Soldier!—
                              A Soldier!—
I want to be a Soldier, with a saber in my hand
Or a little carbine rifle, or a musket on my shoulder,
Or just a snare-drum, snarling in the middle of the band.

I want to see the battle!—

The battle!—

The battle!—

I want to see the battle, and be in it to the end;—
I want to hear the cannon clear their throats and catch the
prattle
Of all the pretty compliments the enemy can send!—
And then I know my wits will go,—and where I *shouldn't*
be—
Well, there's the spot, in any fight, that you may search
for me.

So, when our foes have had their fill.

Though I'm among the dying,

To see The Old Flag flying still,

I'll laugh to leave her flying!

I want to be a Soldier!—

A Soldier!—

A Soldier!—

I want to be a Soldier, with a saber in my hand
Or a little carbine rifle, or a musket on my shoulder,
Or just a snare-drum, snarling in the middle of the band.

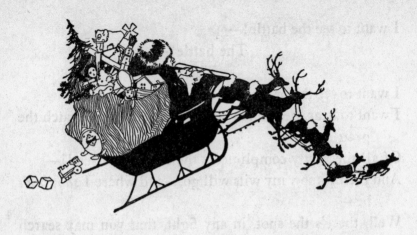

WHAT LITTLE SAUL GOT FOR CHRISTMAS

US PARENTS mostly thinks our own's
    The smartest childern out!
      But widder Shelton's little Saul
Beats all *I* know about!
He's weakly-like—in p'int o' *health,*
    But strong in word and deed
And heart and head, and snap and spunk,
    And allus in the lead!

Come honest' by it, fer his Pa—
    Afore he passed away—
He was a leader—(Lord, I'd like
    To hear him preach to-day!)
He led *his* flock; he led in prayer
    Fer spread o' Peace—and when
Nothin' but *War* could spread it, he
    Was first to lead us *then!*

So little Saul has grit to take
   Things jes as they occur;
And sister Shelton's proud o' him
   As he is proud o' her!
And when she "got up"—jes fer him
   And little playmates all—
A Chris'mus-tree,—they ever'one
   Was there but little Saul.—

Pore little chap was sick in bed
   Next room; and Doc was there,
And said the childern might file past,
   But go right back to where
The *tree* was, in the settin'-room.
   And Saul jes laid and smiled—
Ner couldn't nod, ner wave his hand,
   It hurt so—Bless the child!

And so they left him there with Doc—
   And warm tear of his Ma's. . . . .
Then—suddent-like—high over all
   Their laughture and applause—
They heerd,—"I don't care *what* you git
   On yer old Chris'mus-tree,
'Cause *I'm* got somepin' *you* all haint,—
   I'm got the pleurisy!"

THE ALL-GOLDEN

I

THROUGH every happy line I sing
I feel the tonic of the Spring.
The day is like an old-time face
That gleams across some grassy place—
An old-time face—an old-time chum
Who rises from the grave to come
And lure me back along the ways
Of time's all-golden yesterdays.
Sweet day! to thus remind me of
The truant boy I used to love—
To set, once more, his finger-tips
Against the blossom of his lips,
And pipe for me the signal known
By none but him and me alone!

II

I see, across the schoolroom floor,
The shadow of the open door,
And dancing dust and sunshine blent
Slanting the way the morning went,
And beckoning my thoughts afar
Where reeds and running waters are;

Where amber-colored bayous glass
The half-drown'd weeds and wisps of grass,
Where sprawling frogs, in loveless key,
Sing on and on incessantly.
Against the green wood's dim expanse
The cattail tilts its tufted lance,
While on its tip—one might declare
The white "snake-feeder" blossomed there!

III

I catch my breath, as children do
In woodland swings when life is new,
And all the blood is warm as wine
And tingles with a tang divine.
My soul soars up the atmosphere
And sings aloud where God can hear,
And all my being leans intent
To mark His smiling wonderment.
O gracious dream, and gracious time,
And gracious theme, and gracious rhyme—
When buds of Spring begin to blow
In blossoms that we used to know
And lure us back along the ways
Of time's all-golden yesterdays!

NAUGHTY CLAUDE

WHEN Little Claude was naughty wunst
    At dinner-time, an' said
        He won't say *"Thank you"* to his Ma,
    She maked him go to bed
An' stay two hours an' not git up,—
    So when the clock struck Two,
Nen Claude says,—"Thank you, Mr. Clock,
    I'm much obleeged to you!"

LITTLE MANDY'S CHRISTMAS-TREE

LITTLE Mandy and her Ma
   'S porest folks you ever saw!—
   Lived in porest house in town,
Where the fence 'uz all tore down.

And no front-door steps at all—
Ist a' old box 'g'inst the wall;
And no door-knob on the door
Outside.—*My!* but they 'uz pore!

Wuz no winder-shutters on,
And some of the *winders* gone,
And where *they* 'uz broke they'd pas'e
Ist brown paper 'crost the place.

Tell you! when it's *winter there,*
And the snow ist ever'where,
Little Mandy's Ma she say
'Spec' they'll freeze to death some day.

Wunst my Ma and me—when we
Be'n to church, and's goin' to be
Chris'mus purty soon,—we went
There—like the Committee sent.

And-sir! when we're in the door,
Wuz no carpet on the floor,
And no fire—and heels-and-head
Little Mandy's tucked in bed!

And her Ma telled *my* Ma she
Got no coffee but ist tea,
And fried mush—and's all they had
Sence her health broke down so bad.

Nen Ma hug and hold me where
Little Mandy's layin' there;
And she kiss her, too, and nen
Mandy kiss my Ma again.

And my Ma she telled her *we*
Goin' to have a Chris'mus-Tree,
At the Sund'y School, 'at's fer
ALL the childern, and fer *her*.

Little Mandy *think*—nen she
Say, "What *is* a Chris'mus-Tree?" . .
Nen my Ma she gived *her* Ma
Somepin' 'at I never saw,

And say she *must* take it,—and
She ist maked her keep her hand
Wite close shut,—and nen she *kiss*
Her hand—shut ist like it is.

Nen we comed away. . . . And nen
When it's Chris'mus Eve again,
And all of us childerns be
At the Church and Chris'mus-Tree—

And all git our toys and things
'At old Santy Claus he brings
And puts on the Tree;—wite where
The *big* Tree 'uz standin' there,

And the things 'uz all tooked down,
And the childerns, all in town,
Got their presents—nen we see
They's a *little* Chris'mus-Tree

Wite *behind* the *big* Tree—so
We can't see till *nen,* you know,—
And it's all ist loaded down
With the purtiest things in town!

And the teacher smile and say:
"This-here Tree 'at's hid away
It's marked *'Little Mandy's Tree.'*—
Little Mandy! Where is she?"

Nen nobody say a word.—
Stillest place you ever heard!—
Till a man tiptoe up where
Teacher's still a-waitin' there.

Nen the man he whispers, so
Ist the *Teacher* hears, you know.
Nen he tiptoe back and go
Out the big door—ist as slow!

. . . . . .

Little Mandy, though, *she* don't
Answer—and Ma say "she won't
Never, though each year they'll be
'Little Mandy's Chris'mus-Tree'

Fer pore childern"—my Ma says—
And *Committee* say they guess
"Little Mandy's Tree" 'ull be
Bigger than the *other* Tree!

WET-WEATHER TALK

IT hain't no use to grumble and complane;
  It's jest as cheap and easy to rejoice.—
  When God sorts out the weather and sends rain,
W'y, rain's my choice.

Men ginerly, to all intents—
  Although they're apt to grumble some—
Puts most theyr trust in Providence,
  And takes things as they come—
    That is, the commonality
    Of men that's lived as long as me
    Has watched the world enugh to learn
    They're not the boss of this concern.

With *some,* of course, it's different—
  I've saw *young* men that knowed it all,
And didn't like the way things went
  On this terrestchul ball;—
    But all the same, the rain, some way,
    Rained jest as hard on picnic day;
    Er, when they railly *wanted* it,
    It mayby wouldn't rain a bit!

In this existunce, dry and wet
  Will overtake the best of men—
Some little skift o' clouds'll shet
  The sun off now and then.—

And mayby, whilse you're wundern who
You've fool-like lent your umbrell' to,
And *want* it—out'll pop the sun,
And you'll be glad you hain't got none!

It aggervates the farmers, too—
   They's too much wet, er too much sun,
Er work, er waitin' round to do
   Before the plowin' 's done:
      And mayby, like as not, the wheat,
      Jest as it's lookin' hard to beat,
      Will ketch the storm—and jest about
      The time the corn's a-jintin' out.

These-here *cy-clones* a-foolin' round—
   And back'ard crops!—and wind and rain!—
And yit the corn that's wallerd down
   May elbow up again!—
      They hain't no sense, as I can see,
      Fer mortuls, sich as us, to be
      A-faultin' Natchur's wise intents,
      And lockin' horns with Providence!

It hain't no use to grumble and complane;
   It's jest as cheap and easy to rejoice.—
When God sorts out the weather and sends rain,
   W'y, rain's my choice.

THE LAND OF THUS-AND-SO

"HOW would Willie like to go
To the Land of Thus-and-So?
Everything is proper there—
All the children comb their hair
Smoother than the fur of cats,
Or the nap of high silk hats;
Every face is clean and white
As a lily washed in light;
Never vaguest soil or speck
Found on forehead, throat or neck;
Every little crimpled ear,
In and out, as pure and clear
As the cherry-blossom's blow
In the Land of Thus-and-So.

"Little boys that never fall
Down the stair, or cry at all—
Doing nothing to repent,
Watchful and obedient;
Never hungry, nor in haste—
Tidy shoe-strings always laced;
Never button rudely torn
From its fellows all unworn;
Knickerbockers always new—
Ribbon, tie, and collar, too;
Little watches, worn like men,
Always promptly half-past ten—
Just precisely right, you know,
For the Land of Thus-and-So!

"And the little babies there
Give no one the slightest care—
Nurse has not a thing to do
But be happy and sigh 'Boo!'
While Mamma just nods, and knows
Nothing but to doze and doze:
Never litter round the grate;
Never lunch or dinner late;
Never any household din
Peals without or rings within—
Baby coos nor laughing calls
On the stairs or through the halls—
Just Great Hushes to and fro
Pace the Land of Thus-and-so!

"Oh! the Land of Thus-and-So!—
Isn't it delightful, though?"
"Yes," lisped Willie, answering **me**
Somewhat slow and doubtfully—
"Must be awful nice, but I
Ruther wait till by-and-by
'Fore I go there—maybe when
I be dead I'll go there *then*.—
But"—the troubled little face
Closer pressed in my embrace—
"Le's don't never *ever* go
To the Land of Thus-and-So!"

AT AUNTY'S HOUSE

ONE time, when we'z at Aunty's house—
    'Way in the country!—where
    They's ist but woods—an' pigs, an' cows—
An' all's outdoors an' air!—
An' orchurd-swing; an' churry-trees—
An' *churries* in 'em!—Yes, an' these-
Here redhead birds steals all they please,
    An' tetch 'em ef you dare!—
W'y, wunst, one time, when we wuz there,
    We et out on the porch!

Wite where the cellar-door wuz shut
  The table wuz; an' I
Let Aunty set by me an' cut
  My vittuls up—an' pie.
'Tuz awful funny!—I could see
The redheads in the churry-tree,
An' beehives, where you got to be
  So keerful, goin' by;—
An' "Comp'ny" there an' all!—an' we—
  We et out on the porch!

An' I ist et *p'surves* an' things
  'At Ma don't 'low me to—
An' *chicken-gizzurds*—(don't like *wings*
  Like *Parunts* does! do *you?*)
An' all the time the wind blowed there,
An' I could feel it in my hair,
An' ist smell clover *ever*'where!—
  An' a' old redhead flew
Purt'-nigh wite over my high-chair,
  When we et on the porch!

LITTLE JOHNTS'S CHRIS'MUS

WE got it up a-purpose, jes fer little Johnts,
    you know;
  His mother was so pore an' all, an' had
    to manage so—
Jes bein' a War-widder, an' her pension mighty slim,
She'd take in weavin', er work out, er anything, fer
    him!

An' little Johnts was puny-like, but law, *the nerve* he
    had!—
You'd want to kindo' pity him, but couldn't, very
    bad,—
His pants o' army-blanket an' his coat o' faded blue
Kep' hintin' of his father, like, an' pity wouldn't do!

So we collogued together, onc't, one winter-time, 'at
    we—
Jes me an' mother an' the girls, an' Wilse, John-Jack
    an' Free—
Would jine an' git up little Johnts, by time 'at
    Chris'mus come,
Some sort o' doin's, don't you know, 'at would
    su'prise him some.

An' so, all on the quiet, Mother she turns in an' gits
Some blue-janes—cuts an' makes a suit; an' then sets
     down an' knits
A pair o' little galluses to go 'long with the rest—
An' putts in a red-flannen back, an' buckle on the
     vest.—

The little feller'd be'n so much around our house,
     you see,
An' be'n sich he'p to her an' all, an' handy as could be,
'At Mother couldn't do too much fer little Johnts—
     No, *Sir!*
She ust to jes declare 'at "he was meat-an'-drink to
     her!"

An' Piney, Lide, an' Madaline they watched their
     chance an' rid
To Fountaintown with Lijey's folks; an' bought a
     book, they did,
O' fairy tales, with pictur's in; an' got a little pair
O' red-top boots 'at John-Jack said he'd be'n a-pricin'
     there.

An' Lide got him a little sword, an' Madaline, a
     drum;
An' shootin'-crackers—Lawzy-day! an' they're so
     dangersome!

An' Piney, ever' time the rest 'ud buy some other
toy,
She'd take an' turn in then an' buy more candy fer
the boy!

"Well," thinks-says-I, when they got back, *"your
pocketbooks is dry!"*—
But little Johnts was there hisse'f that afternoon,
so I—
Well, *all* of us kep' mighty mum, tel we got him
away
By tellin' him be shore an' come to-morry—Chris'-
mus Day—

An' fetch *his mother* 'long with him! An' how he
scud acrost
The fields—his towhead, in the dusk, jes like a
streak o' frost!—
His comfert fluttern as he run—an' old Tige, don't
you know,
A-jumpin' high fer rabbits an' a ploughin' up the
snow!

It must 'a' be'n 'most *ten* that night afore we got
to bed—
With Wilse an' John-Jack he'pin' us; an' Freeman
in the shed,

An' Lide out with the lantern while he trimmed the
Chris'mus-Tree
Out of a little scrub-oak-top 'at suited to a "T"!

All night I dreamp' o' hearin' things a-skulkin'
round the place—
An' "Old Kriss," with his whiskers off, an' freckles
on his face—
An' reindeers, shaped like shavin'-hosses at the
cooper-shop,
A-stickin' down the chimbly, with their heels out at
the top!

By time 'at Mother got me up 'twas plum' daylight
an' more—
The front yard full o' neighbers all a-crowdin' round
the door,
With Johnts's mother leadin'; yes—an' little Johnts
hisse'f,
Set up on Freeman's shoulder, like a jug up on the
she'f!

Of course I can't describe it when they all got in
to where
We'd conjered up the Chris'mus-Tree an' all the
fixin's there!—
Fer all the shouts o' laughture—clappin' hands, an'
crackin' jokes,
Was heap o' kissin' goin' on amongst the women-
folks:—

Fer, lo-behold-ye! there they had that young-un!—
　　An' his chin
A-wobblin'-like;—an', shore enough, at last he
　　started in—
An'—sich another bellerin', in all my mortal days,
I never heerd, er 'spect to hear, in woe's app'inted
　　ways!

An' Mother grabs him up an' says: "It's more'n he
　　can bear—
It's all too *suddent* fer the child, an' too su'prisin'!
　　—*There!*"
"Oh, no it ain't"—sobbed little Johnts—"I ain't
　　su'prised—but I'm
A-cryin' 'cause I watched you all, an' knowed it **all**
　　the time!"

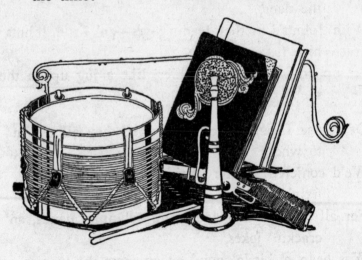

OUR KIND OF A MAN

I

THE kind of a man for you and me!
　　He faces the world unflinchingly,
　　And smites, as long as the wrong resists,
With a knuckled faith and force like fists:
He lives the life he is preaching of,
And loves where most is the need of love;
His voice is clear to the deaf man's ears,
And his face sublime through the blind man's tears;
The light shines out where the clouds were dim,
And the widow's prayer goes up for him;
The latch is clicked at the hovel door
And the sick man sees the sun once more,
And out o'er the barren fields he sees
Springing blossoms and waving trees,
Feeling as only the dying may,
That God's own servant has come that way,
Smoothing the path as it still winds on
Through the golden gate where his loved have gone.

171

The kind of a man for me and you!
However little of worth we do
He credits full, and abides in trust
That time will teach us how more is just.
He walks abroad, and he meets all kinds
Of querulous and uneasy minds,
And, sympathizing, he shares the pain
Of the doubts that rack us, heart and brain;
And, knowing this, as we grasp his hand,
We are surely coming to understand!
He looks on sin with pitying eyes—
E'en as the Lord, since Paradise,—
Else, should we read, Though our sins should glow
As scarlet, they shall be white as snow?—
And, feeling still, with a grief half glad,
That the bad are as good as the good are bad,
He strikes straight out for the Right—and he
Is the kind of a man for you and me!

WHEN THE WORLD BU'STS THROUGH

WHERE'S a boy a-goin',
 An' what's he goin' to do,
 An' how's he goin' to do it,
When the world bu'sts through?
Ma she says "she can't tell
 What we're comin' to!"
An' Pop says "he's ist skeered
 Clean—plum—through!"

S'pose we'd be a-playin'
 Out in the street,
An' the ground 'ud split up
 'Bout forty feet!—
Ma says "she ist knows
 We 'ud tumble in";
An' Pop says "he bets you
 Nen we wouldn't grin!"

173

S'pose we ist be 'tendin'
　　Like we had a show,
Down in the stable,
　　Where we mustn't go,—
Ma says, "The earthquake
　　Might make it fall";
An' Pop says, "More'n like
　　Swaller barn an' all!"

Landy! ef we both wuz
　　Runnin' 'way from school,
Out in the shady woods
　　Where it's all so cool!—
Ma says "a big tree
　　Might sqush our head";
An' Pop says, "Chop 'em out
　　Both—killed—dead!"

But where's a boy goin',
　　And what's he goin' to do,
An' how's he goin' to do it,
　　Ef the world bu'sts through?
Ma she says "she can't tell
　　What we're comin' to!"
An' Pop says "he's ist skeered
　　Clean—plum—through!"

THE BEAR STORY

THAT ALEX "IST MAKED UP HIS-OWN-SE'F"

W'Y, wunst they wuz a Little Boy went out
In the woods to shoot a Bear. So, he
went out
'Way in the grea'-big woods—he did.—An' he
Wuz goin' along—an' goin' along, you know,
An' purty soon he heerd somepin' go *"Wooh!"*—
Ist thataway—*"Woo-ooh!"* An' he wuz *skeered,*
He wuz. An' so he runned an' clumbed a tree—
A grea'-big tree, he did,—a sicka-*more* tree.
An' nen he heerd it ag'in: an' he looked round,
An' *'t'uz a Bear!—a grea'-big shore-nuff Bear!*—
No: 't'uz *two* Bears, it wuz—two grea'-big Bears—
One of 'em wuz—ist *one'z* a *grea'-big* Bear.—
But they ist *boff* went *"Wooh!"*—An' here *they* come
To climb the tree an' git the Little Boy
An' eat him up!

An' nen the Little Boy
He 'uz skeered worse'n ever! An' here come

The grea'-big Bear a-climbin' th' tree to git
The Little Boy an' eat him up—Oh, *no!*—
It 'uzn't the *Big* Bear 'at clumb the tree—
It 'uz the *Little* Bear. So here *he* come
Climbin' the tree—an' climbin' the tree! Nen when
He git wite *clos't* to the Little Boy, w'y nen
The Little Boy he ist pulled up his gun
An' *shot* the Bear, he did, an' killed him dead!
An' nen the Bear he falled clean on down out
The tree—away clean to the ground, he did—
Spling-splung! he falled *plum'* down, an' killed him,
        too!
An' lit wite side o' where the *Big* Bear's at.

An' nen the Big Bear's awful mad, you bet!—
'Cause—'cause the Little Boy he shot his gun
An' killed the *Little* Bear.—'Cause the *Big* Bear
He—he 'uz the Little Bear's Papa.—An' so here
He come to climb the big old tree an' git
The Little Boy an' eat him up! An' when
The Little Boy he saw the *grea'-big Bear*
A-comin', he 'uz badder skeered, he wuz,
Than *any* time! An' so he think he'll climb
Up *higher*—'way up higher in the tree
Than the old *Bear* kin climb, you know.—But he—
He *can't* climb higher 'an old *Bears* kin climb,—
'Cause Bears kin climb up higher in the trees
Than any little Boys in all the Wo-r-r-ld!

An' so here come the grea'-big Bear, he did,—
A-climbin' up—an' up the tree, to git
The Little Boy an' eat him up! An' so
The Little Boy he clumbed on higher, an' higher,
An' higher up the tree—an' higher—an' higher—
An' higher'n iss-here *house* is!—An' here come
Th' old Bear—clos'ter to him all the time!—
An' nen—first thing you know,—when th' old Big
      Bear
Wuz wite clos't to him—nen the Little Boy
Ist jabbed his gun wite in the old Bear's mouf
An' shot an' killed him dead!—No; I *fergot,*—
He didn't shoot the grea'-big Bear at all—
'Cause *they 'uz no load in the gun,* you know—
'Cause when he shot the *Little* Bear, w'y, nen
No load 'uz anymore nen *in* the gun!

But th' Little Boy clumbed *higher* up, he did—
He clumbed *lots* higher—an' on up *higher*—an' higher
An' *higher*—tel he ist *can't* climb no higher,
'Cause nen the limbs 'uz all so little, 'way
Up in the teeny-weeny tip-top of
The tree, they'd break down wiv him ef he don't
Be keerful! So he stop an' think: An' nen
He look around—*An' here come th' old Bear!*

An' so the Little Boy make up his mind
He's got to ist git out o' there *some* way!—

177

'Cause here come the old Bear!—so clos't, his bref's
Purt' nigh so's he kin feel how hot it is
Ag'inst his bare feet—ist like old "Ring's" bref
When he's ben out a-huntin' an's all tired.
So when th' old Bear's so clos't—the Little Boy
Ist gives a grea'-big jump fer *'nother* tree—
No!—no he don't do that!—I tell you what
The Little Boy does:—W'y, nen—w'y, he—Oh, *yes*—
The Little Boy *he finds a hole up there*
'At's in the tree—an' climbs in there an' *hides*—
An' *nen* th' old Bear can't find the Little Boy
At all!—But, purty soon th' old Bear finds
The Little Boy's *gun* 'at's up there—'cause the *gun*
It's too *tall* to tooked wiv him in the hole.
So, when the old Bear fin' the *gun,* he knows
The Little Boy's ist *hid* 'round *somers* there,—
An' th' old Bear 'gins to snuff an' sniff around,
An' sniff an' snuff around—so's he kin find
Out where the Little Boy's hid at.—An' nen—nen—
Oh, *yes!*—W'y, purty soon the old Bear climbs
'Way out on a big limb—a grea'-long limb,—
An' nen the Little Boy climbs out the hole
An' takes his ax an' chops the limb off! . . . Nen
The old Bear falls *k-splunge!* clean to the ground
An' bust an' kill hisse'f plum' dead, he did!

An' nen the Little Boy he git his gun
An' 'menced a-climbin' down the tree ag'in—

No!—no, he *didn't* git his *gun*—'cause when
The *Bear* falled, nen the *gun* falled, too—An' broked
It all to pieces, too!—An' *nicest* gun!—
His Pa ist buyed it!—An' the Little Boy
Ist cried, he did; an' went on climbin' down
The tree—an' climbin' down—an' climbin' down!—
An'-sir! when he 'uz purt'-nigh down,—w'y, nen
The old Bear he jumped up ag'in!—an' he
Ain't dead at all—ist *'tendin'* thataway,
So he kin git the Little Boy an' eat
Him up! But the Little Boy he 'uz too smart
To climb clean *down* the tree.—An' the old Bear
He can't climb *up* the tree no more—'cause when
He fell, he broke one of his—he broke *all*
His legs!—an' nen he *couldn't* climb! But he
Ist won't go 'way an' let the Little Boy
Come down out of the tree. An' the old Bear
Ist growls 'round there, he does—ist growls an' goes
"Wooh!—Woo-ooh!" all the time! An' Little Boy
He haf to stay up in the tree—all night—
An' 'thout no *supper* neether!—On'y they
Wuz *apples* on the tree!—An' Little Boy
Et apples—ist all night—an' cried—an' cried!
Nen when 't'uz morning th' old Bear went *"Wooh!"*
Ag'in, an' try to climb up in the tree
An' git the Little Boy.—But he *can't*
Climb t'save his *soul,* he can't!—An' *oh!* he's *mad!*—
He ist tear up the ground! an' go *"Woo-ooh!"*

An'—*Oh, yes!*—purty soon, when morning's come
All *light*—so's you kin *see,* you know,—w'y, nen
The old Bear finds the Little Boy's *gun,* you know,
'At's on the ground.—(An' it ain't broke at all—
I ist *said* that!) An' so the old Bear think
He'll take the gun an' *shoot* the Little Boy:—
But *Bears they* don't know much 'bout shootin' guns;
So when he go to shoot the Little Boy,
The old Bear got the *other* end the gun
Ag'in' his shoulder, 'stid o' *th'other* end—
So when he try to shoot the Little Boy,
It shot *the Bear,* it did—an' killed him dead!
An' nen the Little Boy clumb down the tree
An' chopped his old woolly head off:—Yes, an' killed
The *other* Bear ag'in, he did—an' killed
All *boff* the bears, he did—an' tuk 'em home
An' *cooked* 'em, too, an' *et* 'em!
                                        —An' that's all.

ON THE SUNNY SIDE

HI and whoop-hooray, boys!
    Sing a song of cheer!
    Here's a holiday, boys,
  Lasting half a year!
Round the world, and half is
    Shadow we have tried;
Now we're where the laugh is,—
    On the sunny side!

Pigeons coo and mutter,
    Strutting high aloof
Where the sunbeams flutter
    Through the stable roof.
Hear the chickens cheep, boys,
    And the hen with pride
Clucking them to sleep, boys,
    On the sunny side!

Hear the clacking guinea;
    Hear the cattle moo;
Hear the horses whinny,
    Looking out at you!

On the hitching-block, boys,
  Grandly satisfied,
See the old peacock, boys,
  On the sunny side!

Robins in the peach tree;
  Bluebirds in the pear;
Blossoms over each tree
  In the orchard there!
All the world's in joy, boys,
  Glad and glorified
As a romping boy, boys,
  On the sunny side!

Where's a heart as mellow—
  Where's a soul as free—
Where is any fellow
  We would rather be?
Just ourselves or none, boys,
  World around and wide,
Laughing in the sun, boys,
  On the sunny side!

'LIZABUTH-ANN ON BAKIN'-DAY

OUR Hired Girl, when it's bakin'-day
    She's out o' patience allus,
  An' tells us "Hike *outdoors* an' play,
An' when the cookies's done," she'll say,
  "Land sake! she'll come an' call us!"
An' when the little doughbowl's all
Ist heapin'-full, she'll come an' call—
  Nen say, "She ruther take a switchin'
Than have a pack o' pesky childern
  Trackin' round the kitchen!"

PRIOR TO MISS BELLE'S APPEARANCE

WHAT makes you come *here* fer, Mister,
　　So much to *our* house?—*Say?*
　　Come to see our big sister?—
An' Charley he says 'at you kissed her
　　An' he ketched you, th' uther day!—
Didn' you, Charley?—But we p'omised Belle
An' crossed our heart to never to tell—
'Cause *she* gived us some o' them-er
Chawk'lut drops 'at you bringed to her!

Charley he's my little b'uther—
　　An' we has a-mostest fun,
Don't we, Charley?—Our Muther,
Whenever we whips one anuther,
　　Tries to whip *us*—an' we *run*—
Don't we, Charley?—An' nen, bime-by,
Nen she gives us cake—an' pie—
Don't she, Charley?—when we come in
An' p'omise never to do it ag'in?

He's named Charley.—I'm *Willie*—
　An' I'm got the purtiest name!
But Uncle Bob *he* calls me "Billy"—
Don't he, Charley?—'N' our filly
　We named "Billy," the same
Ist like me! An' our Ma said
'At "Bob puts foolishnuss into our head!"—
Didn' she, Charley?—An' *she* don't know
Much about *boys!*—'Cause Bob said so!

Baby's a funniest feller!
　Nain't no hair on his head—
Is they, Charley?—It's meller
Wite up there! An' ef Belle er
　Us ask wuz *we* that way, Ma said,—
"Yes; an' yer *Pa's* head wuz soft as that,
An' it's that way yet!"—An' Pa grabs his hat
An' says, "Yes, childern, she's right about Pa—
'Cause that's the reason he married yer Ma!"

An' our Ma says 'at "Belle couldn'
　Ketch nothin' at all but ist *'bows' !*"—
An' *Pa* says 'at "you're soft as puddun!"—
An' *Uncle Bob* says "you're a good-un
　'Cause he can tell by yer nose!"—
Didn' he, Charley?—An' when Belle'll play
In the poller on th' pianer, some day,
Bob makes up funny songs about you,
Till she gits mad—like he wants her to!

Our sister *Fanny* she's *'leven*
    Years old! 'At's mucher 'an *I*—
Ain't it, Charley? . . . I'm seven!—
But our sister Fanny's in *Heaven!*
    Nere's where you go ef you die!—
Don't you, Charley?—Nen you has *wings*—
Ist like Fanny!—an' *purtiest things!*—
Don't you, Charley?—An' nen you can fly—
Ist fly—an' *ever*'thing! . . . Wisht *I'd* die!

JACK THE GIANT-KILLER
BAD BOY'S VERSION

TELL you a story—an' it's a fac':—
   Wunst wuz a little boy, name wuz Jack,
   An' he had sword an' buckle an' strap
Maked of gold, an' a " 'visibul cap";
An' he killed Gi'nts 'at et whole cows—
Th' horns an' all—an' pigs an' sows!
But Jack, his golding sword wuz, oh!
So awful sharp 'at he could go
An' cut th' old Gi'nts clean in two
'Fore 'ey knowed what he wuz goin' to do!

An' *one* ole Gi'nt, he had four
Heads, an' name wuz "Bumblebore"—
An' he wuz feared o' Jack—'cause he,
Jack, he killed six—five—ten-three,
An' all o' th' uther Gi'nts but him:
An' thay wuz a place Jack haf to swim
'Fore he could git t' ole "Bumblebore"—
Nen thay wuz "griffuns" at the door:
But Jack, he thist plunged in an' swum
Clean acrost; an' when he come
To th' uther side, he thist put on
His " 'visibul cap," an' nen, dog-gone!
You couldn't see him at all!—An' so
He slewed the "griffuns"—*boff,* you know!
Nen wuz a horn hunged over his head,
High on th' wall, an' words 'at read,—
"Whoever kin this trumpet blow
Shall cause the Gi'nt's overth'ow!"
An' Jack, he thist reached up an' blowed
The stuffin' out of it! an' th'owed
Th' castul gates wide open, an'
Nen tuk his gold sword in his han',
An' thist marched in t' ole "Bumblebore,"
An', 'fore he knowed, he put 'bout four
Heads on him—an' chopped 'em off, too!—
Wisht 'at *I'd* been Jack!—don't you?

UNCLE he learns us to rhyme an' write
An' all be poets an' all recite:
His little-est poet's his little-est niece,
An' this is her little-est poetry-piece.

AN OLD SWEETHEART OF MINE

AN Old Sweetheart of Mine!—is this her presence
        here with me,
    Or but a vain creation of a lover's memory?
A fair, illusive vision that would vanish into air
Dared I even touch the silence with the whisper of a
    prayer? ·

Nay, let me then believe in all the blended false and
    true—
The semblance of the *old* love and the substance of the
    new,—
The *then* of changeless sunny days—the *now* of shower
    and shine—
But Love forever smiling,—as that old sweetheart of
    mine.

This ever-restful sense of *home,* though shouts ring in the
    hall.—
The easy-chair—the old bookshelves and prints along the
    wall;
The rare *Habanas* in their box, or gaunt churchwarden-
    stem
That often wags, above the jar, derisively at them.

As one who cons at evening o'er an album, all alone,
And muses on the faces of the friends that he has known,
So I turn the leaves of Fancy, till, in shadowy design,
I find the smiling features of an old sweetheart of mine.

The lamplight seems to glimmer with a flicker of surprise,
As I turn it low—to rest me of the dazzle in my eyes,
And light my pipe in silence, save a sigh that seems to
    yoke
Its fate with my tobacco and to vanish with the smoke.

'Tis a *fragrant* retrospection,—for the loving thoughts
    that start
Into being are like perfume from the blossom of the heart;
And to dream the old dreams over is a luxury divine—
When my truant fancies wander with that old sweetheart
    of mine.

Though I hear beneath my study, like a fluttering of
    wings,
The voices of my children and the mother as she sings—
I feel no twinge of conscience to deny me any theme
When Care has cast her anchor in the harbor of a dream—

In fact, to speak in earnest, I believe it adds a charm
To spice the good a trifle with a little dust of harm,—
For I find an extra flavor in Memory's mellow wine
That makes me drink the deeper to that old sweetheart of
    mine.

O Childhood-days enchanted! O the magic of the
    Spring!—
With all green boughs to blossom white, and all bluebirds
    to sing!
When all the air, to toss and quaff, made life a jubilee
And changed the children's song and laugh to shrieks of
    ecstasy.

With eyes half closed in clouds that ooze from lips that
    taste, as well,
The peppermint and cinnamon, I hear the old School-bell,
And from "Recess" romp in again from "Blackman's"
    broken line,
To—smile, behind my "lesson," at that old sweetheart of
    mine.

A face of lily-beauty, with a form of airy grace,
Floats out of my tobacco as the "Genii" from the vase;
And I thrill beneath the glances of a pair of azure eyes
As glowing as the summer and as tender as the skies.

I can see the pink sunbonnet and the little, checkered dress
She wore when first I kissed her and she answered the caress
With the written declaration that, "As surely as the vine
Grew 'round the stump," she loved me—that old sweet-
    heart of mine.

Again I make her presents, in a really helpless way,—
The big "Rhode Island Greening"—(I was hungry too,
    that day!)—
But I follow her from Spelling, with her hand behind
    her—so—
And I slip the apple in it—and the Teacher doesn't know!

I give my *treasures* to her—all,—my pencil—blue-and-
    red;—
And, if little girls played marbles, *mine* should all be *hers*
    instead!—
But *she* gave me her *photograph,* and printed "Ever Thine"
Across the back—in blue-and-red—that old sweetheart of
    mine!

And again I feel the pressure of her slender little hand,
As we used to talk together of the future we had
    planned,—
When I should be a poet, and with nothing else to do
But write the tender verses that she set the music to. . . .

When we should live together in a cozy little cot
Hid in a nest of roses, with a fairy garden-spot,
Where the vines were ever fruited and the weather ever
    fine,
And the birds were ever singing for that old sweetheart of
    mine. . . .

When I should be her lover forever and a day,
And she my faithful sweetheart till the golden hair was
    gray;
And we should be so happy that when either's lips were
    dumb
They would not smile in Heaven till the other's kiss had
    come.

But, ah! my dream is broken by a step upon the stair,
And the door is softly opened, and—my wife is standing
    there:
Yet with eagerness and rapture all my visions I resign,—
To greet the *living* presence of that old sweetheart of
    mine.

THE POEMS HERE AT HOME

THE Poems here at Home!—Who'll write 'em
    down,
    Jes' as they air—in Country and in Town?
Sowed thick as clods is 'crost the fields and lanes,
Er these-'ere little hop-toads when it rains!—
Who'll "voice" 'em? as I heerd a feller say
'At speechified on Freedom, t'other day,
And soared the Eagle tel, it 'peared to me,
She wasn't bigger'n a bumble-bee!

Who'll sort 'em out and set 'em down, says I,
'At's got a stiddy hand enough to try
To do 'em jestice 'thout a-foolin' some,
And headin' facts off when they want to come?—
Who's got the lovin' eye, and heart, and brain
To reco'nize 'at nothin's made in vain—
'At the Good Bein' made the bees and birds
And brutes first choice, and us-folks afterwards?

What We want, as I sense it, in the line
O' poetry is somepin' Yours and Mine—
Somepin' with live stock in it, and out-doors,
And old crick-bottoms, snags, and sycamores:
Putt weeds in—pizen-vines, and underbresh,
As well as johnny-jump-ups, all so fresh
And sassy-like!—and groun'-squir'ls,—yes, and "We,"
As sayin' is,—"We, Us and Company!"

Putt in old Nature's sermonts,—them's the best,—
And 'casion'ly hang up a hornets' nest
'At boys 'at's run away from school can git
At handy-like—and let 'em tackle it!
Let us be wrought on, of a truth, to feel
Our proneness fer to hurt more than we heal,
In ministratin' to our vain delights—
Fergittin' even insec's has their rights!

No "Ladies' Amaranth," ner "Treasury" book—
Ner "Night Thoughts," nuther—ner no "Lally Rook"!
We want some poetry 'at's to Our taste,
Made out o' truck 'at's jes' a-goin' to waste
'Cause smart folks thinks it's altogether too
Outrageous common—'cept fer me and you!—
Which goes to argy, all sich poetry
Is 'bliged to rest its hopes on You and Me.

195

OLD OCTOBER

OLD October's purt' nigh gone,
  And the frosts is comin' on
  Little *heavier* every day—
Like our hearts is thataway!
Leaves is changin' overhead
Back from green to gray and red
Brown and yeller, with their stems
Loosenin' on the oaks and e'ms;
And the balance of the trees
Gittin' balder every breeze—
Like the heads we're scratchin' on!
Old October's purt' nigh gone.

I love Old October so,
I can't bear to see her go—
Seems to me like losin' some
Old-home relative er chum—
'Pears like sort o' settin' by
Some old friend 'at sigh by sigh
Was a-passin' out o' sight
Into everlastin' night!

Hickernuts a feller hears
Rattlin' down is more like tears
Drappin' on the leaves below—
I love Old October so!

Can't tell what it is about
Old October knocks me out!—
I sleep well enough at night—
And the blamedest appetite
Ever mortal man possessed,—
Last thing et, it tastes the best!—
Warnuts, butternuts, pawpaws,
'Iles and limbers up my jaws
Fer raal service, sich as new
Pork, spareribs, and sausage, too.—
Yit, fer all, they's somepin' 'bout
Old October knocks me out!

THE TREE-TOAD

"SCUR'OUS-LIKE," said the tree-toad,
  "I've twittered fer rain all day;
    And I got up soon,
    And hollered tel noon—
But the sun, hit blazed away,
    Tel I jest clumb down in a crawfish-hole,
    Weary at hart, and sick at soul!

"Dozed away fer an hour,
    And I tackled the thing ag'in:
    And I sung, and sung,
    Tel I knowed my lung
Was jest about give in;
    And *then*, thinks I, ef hit don't rain *now*,
    They's nothin' in singin', anyhow!

"Onc't in a while some farmer
    Would come a-drivin' past;
        And he'd hear my cry,
        And stop and sigh—
    Tel I jest laid back, at last,
        And I hollered rain tel I thought my th'oat
        Would bust wide open at ever' note!

"But I *fetched* her!—O *I fetched* her!—
    'Cause a little while ago,
        As I kindo' set,
        With one eye shet,
    And a-singin' soft and low,
        A voice drapped down on my fevered brain,
        A-sayin',—'*Ef you'll jest hush I'll rain!*' "

A BAREFOOT BOY

A BAREFOOT boy! I mark him at his play—
  For May is here once more, and so is he,—
  His dusty trousers, rolled half to the knee,
And his bare ankles grimy, too, as they:
Cross-hatchings of the nettle, in array
 Of feverish stripes, hint vividly to me
 Of woody pathways winding endlessly
Along the creek, where even yesterday
He plunged his shrinking body—gasped and shook—
 Yet called the water "warm," with never lack
Of joy. And so, half enviously I look
 Upon this graceless barefoot and his track,—
 His toe stubbed—ay, his big toe-nail knocked back
Like unto the clasp of an old pocketbook.

A COUNTRY PATHWAY

I COME upon it suddenly, alone—
    A little pathway winding in the weeds
    That fringe the roadside; and with dreams my
       own,
  I wander as it leads.

Full wistfully along the slender way,
    Through summer tan of freckled shade and shine,
I take the path that leads me as it may—
    Its every choice is mine.

A chipmunk, or a sudden-whirring quail,
    Is startled by my step as on I fare—
A garter-snake across the dusty trail
    Glances and—is not there.

Above the arching jimson-weeds flare twos
    And twos of sallow-yellow butterflies,
Like blooms of lorn primroses blowing loose
    When autumn winds arise.

The trail dips—dwindles—broadens then, and lifts
    Itself astride a cross-road dubiously,
And, from the fennel marge beyond it, drifts
    Still onward, beckoning me.

And though it needs must lure me mile on mile
    Out of the public highway, still I go,
My thoughts, far in advance in Indian-file,
    Allure me even so.

Why, I am as a long-lost boy that went
    At dusk to bring the cattle to the bars,
And was not found again, though Heaven lent
    His mother all the stars

With which to seek him through that awful night.
    O years of nights as vain!—Stars never rise
But well might miss their glitter in the light
    Of tears in mother-eyes!

So—on, with quickened breaths, I follow still—
    My avant-courier must be obeyed!
Thus am I led, and thus the path, at will,
    Invites me to invade

A meadow's precincts, where my daring guide
    Clambers the steps of an old-fashioned stile,
And stumbles down again, the other side,
    To gambol there awhile

In pranks of hide-and-seek, as on ahead
    I see it running, while the clover-stalks
Shake rosy fists at me, as though they said—
    "You dog our country-walks

"And mutilate us with your walking-stick!—
    We will not suffer tamely what you do,
And warn you at your peril,—for we'll sic
    Our bumblebees on you!"

But I smile back, in airy nonchalance,—
    The more determined on my wayward quest,
As some bright memory a moment dawns
    A morning in my breast—

Sending a thrill that hurries me along
    In faulty similes of childish skips,
Enthused with lithe contortions of a song
    Performing on my lips.

In wild meanderings o'er pasture wealth—
    Erratic wanderings through dead'ning-lands,
Where sly old brambles, plucking me by stealth,
    Put berries in my hands:

Or the path climbs a boulder—wades a slough—
    Or, rollicking through buttercups and flags,
Goes gaily dancing o'er a deep bayou
    On old tree-trunks and snags:

Or, at the creek, leads o'er a limpid pool
    Upon a bridge the stream itself has made,
With some Spring-freshet for the mighty tool
    That its foundation laid.

I pause a moment here to bend and muse,
    With dreamy eyes, on my reflection, where
A boat-backed bug drifts on a helpless cruise,
    Or wildly oars the air,

As, dimly seen, the pirate of the brook—
    The pike, whose jaunty hulk denotes his speed—
Swings pivoting about, with wary look
    Of low and cunning greed.

Till, filled with other thought, I turn again
    To where the pathway enters in a realm
Of lordly woodland, under sovereign reign
    Of towering oak and elm.

A puritanic quiet here reviles
    The almost whispered warble from the hedge,
And takes a locust's rasping voice and files
    The silence to an edge.

In such a solitude my somber way
    Strays like a misanthrope within a gloom
Of his own shadows—till the perfect day
    Bursts into sudden bloom,

And crowns a long, declining stretch of space,
    Where King Corn's armies lie with flags unfurled,
And where the valley's dint in Nature's face
    Dimples a smiling world.

And lo! through mists that may not be dispelled,
    I see an old farm homestead, as in dreams,
Where, like a gem in costly setting held,
    The old log cabin gleams.

. . . .

O darling Pathway! lead me bravely on
    Adown your valley-way, and run before
Among the roses crowding up the lawn
    And thronging at the door,—

And carry up the echo there that shall
    Arouse the drowsy dog, that he may bay
The household out to greet the prodigal
    That wanders home to-day.

A FEW OF THE BIRD-FAMILY

THE Old Bob-white, and Chipbird;
   The Flicker, and Chewink,
   And little hopty-skip bird
Along the river-brink.

The Blackbird, and Snowbird,
   The Chicken-hawk, and Crane;
The glossy old black Crow-bird,
   And Buzzard down the lane.

The Yellowbird, and Redbird,
   The Tomtit, and the Cat;
The Thrush, and that Red*head*-bird
   The rest's all pickin' at!

The Jay-bird, and the Bluebird,
   The Sapsuck, and the Wren—
The Cockadoodle-doo-bird,
   And our old Settin'-hen!

A FULL HARVEST

SEEMS like a feller'd ort'o jes' to-day
    Git down and roll and waller, don't you know,
    In that-air stubble, and flop up and crow,
Seein' sich crops! I'll undertake to say
There're no wheat's ever turned out thataway
 Afore this season!—Folks is keerless, though,
    And too fergitful—'caze we'd ort'o show
More thankfulness!—Jes' looky hyonder, hey?—
    And watch that little reaper wadin' thue
That last old yaller hunk o' harvest-ground—
    Jes' natchur'ly a-slicin' it in two
Like honeycomb, and gaumin' it around
    The field—like it had nothin' else to do
    On'y jes' waste it all on me and you!

RIGHT HERE AT HOME

RIGHT here at home, boys, in old Hoosierdom,
　　Where strangers allus joke us when they come
　　And brag o' *their* old States and interprize—
Yit *settle* here; and 'fore they realize,
They're "hoosier" as the rest of us, and live
Right here at home, boys, with their past fergive'!

Right here at home, boys, is the place, I guess,
Fer me and you and plain old happiness:
We hear the World's lots grander—likely so,—
We'll take the World's word fer it and not go.—
We know *its* ways ain't *our* ways—so we'll stay
Right here at home, boys, where we *know* the way.

Right here at home, boys, where a well-to-do
Man's plenty rich enough—and knows it, too,
And's got a' extry dollar, any time,
To boost a feller up 'at *wants* to climb
And's got the git-up in him to go in
And *git there*, like he purt' nigh allus kin!

Right here at home, boys, is the place fer us!—
Where folks' heart's bigger'n their money-pu's';
And where a *common* feller's jes' as good
As ary other in the neighberhood:
The World at large don't worry you and me
Right here at home, boys, where we ort to be!

Right here at home, boys—jes' right where we air!—
Birds don't sing any sweeter anywhere:
Grass don't grow any greener'n she grows
Across the pastur' where the old path goes,—
All things in ear-shot's purty, er in sight,
Right here at home, boys, ef we *size* 'em right.

Right here at home, boys, where the old home-place
Is sacerd to us as our mother's face,
Jes' as we rickollect her, last she smiled
And kissed us—dyin' so and rickonciled,
Seein' us all at home here—none astray—
Right here at home, boys, where she sleeps to-day.

OLD WINTERS ON THE FARM

I HAVE jest about decided
It 'ud keep a *town-boy* hoppin'
Fer to work all winter, choppin'
Fer a' old fireplace, like *I* did!
Lawz! them old times wuz contrairy!—
    Blame' backbone o' winter, 'peared-like
    Wouldn't break!—and I wuz skeerd-like
Clean on into *Feb'uary!*
    Nothin' ever made me madder
Than fer Pap to stomp in, layin'
On a' extra fore-stick, sayin'
    "Groun'-hog's out and seed his shadder!"

THE OLD HOME BY THE MILL

THIS is "The old Home by the Mill"—fer we
    still call it so,
    Although the *old mill*, roof and sill, is all gone
    long ago.
The old home, though, and old folks—and the old spring,
    and a few
Old cattails, weeds and hartychokes, is left to welcome
    you!

Here, Marg'et, fetch the man a tin to drink out of! Our
    spring
Keeps kindo'-sorto' cavin' in, but don't "*taste*" anything!
She's kindo' *agin'*, Marg'et is—"the *old* process," like
    me,
All ham-stringed up with rhumatiz, and on in seventy-
    three.

Jes' me and Marg'et lives alone here—like in long ago;
The childern all putt off and gone, and married, don't
    you know?

One's millin' way out West somewhare; two other miller-boys
In Minnyopolis they air; and one's in Illinoise.

The *oldest* gyrl—the first that went—married and died right here;
The next lives in Winn's Settlement—for purt' nigh thirty year!
And youngest one—was allus fer the old home here— but no!—
Her man turns in and packs *her* 'way off to Idyho!

I don't miss them like *Marg'et* does—'cause I got *her*, you see;
And when she pines for them—that's 'cause *she's* only jes' got *me!*
I laugh, and joke her 'bout it all.—But talkin' sense, I'll say,
When she was tuk so bad last Fall, I laughed then t'other way!

I hain't so favor'ble impressed 'bout *dyin'*; but ef I
Found I was only second-best when *us two* come to die,
I'd 'dopt the "new process," in full, ef *Marg'et* died, you see,—
I'd jes' crawl in my grave and pull the green grass over me!

SOMEP'N COMMON-LIKE

SOMEP'N 'at's common-like, and good
And plain, and easy understood;
Somep'n 'at folks like me and you
Kin understand, and relish, too,
And find some sermint in 'at hits
The spot, and sticks and benefits.

We don't need nothin' extry fine;
'Cause, take the run o' minds like mine,
And we'll go more on good horse-sense
Than all your flowery eloquence;
And we'll jedge best of honest acts
By Nature's statement of the facts.

So when you're wantin' to express
Your misery, er happiness,
Er anything 'at's wuth the time
O' telling in plain talk er rhyme—
Jes' sort o' let your subject run
As ef the Lord wuz listenun.

WRITIN' BACK TO THE HOME-FOLKS

M Y dear old friends—It jes' beats all,
     The way you write a letter
     So's ever' *last* line beats the *first*,
And ever' *next*-un's better!—
W'y, ever' fool-thing you putt down
     You make so inte*rest*in',
A feller, readin' of 'em all,
     Can't tell which is the *best*-un.

It's all so comfortin' and good,
     'Pears-like I almost *hear* ye
And git more sociabler, you know,
     And hitch my cheer up near ye
And jes' smile on ye like the sun
     Acrosst the whole per-rairies
In Aprile when the thaw's begun
     And country couples marries.

It's all so good-old-fashioned like
    To *talk* jes' like we're *thinkin'*,
Without no hidin' back o' fans
    And giggle-un and winkin',
Ner sizin' how each other's dressed——
    Like some is allus doin'——
"*Is* Marthy Ellen's basque be'n *turned*
    Er shore-enough a new-un!"——

Er "ef Steve's city-friend hain't jes'
    'A *lee*tle kind o' sort o' ' "——
Er "wears them-air blame' eye-glasses
    Jes' 'cause he hadn't ort to?"——
And so straight on, *dad-libitum*,
    Tel all of us feels, *some*way,
Jes' like our "comp'ny" wuz the best
    When we git up to come 'way!

That's why I like *old* friends like you,——
    Jes' 'cause you're so *abidin'*.——
Ef I was built to live "*fer keeps*,"
    My principul residin'
Would be amongst the folks 'at kep'
    Me allus *thinkin'* of 'em
And sort o' eechin' all the time
    To tell 'em how I love 'em.——

Sich folks, you know, I jes' love so
    I wouldn't live without 'em,
Er couldn't even drap asleep
    But what I *dreamp'* about 'em,—
And ef we minded God, I guess
    We'd *all* love one another
Jes' like one famb'ly,—me and Pap
    And Madaline and Mother.

AT "THE LITERARY"

FOLKS in town, I reckon, thinks
　　They git all the fun they air
　　Runnin' loose 'round!—but, 'y jinks!
We' got fun, and fun to spare,
Right out here amongst the ash-
　　And oak-timber ever'where!
Some folks else kin cut a dash
　　'Sides town-people, don't fergit!—
'Specially in *winter*-time,
　　When they's snow, and roads is fit.
In them circumstances I'm
　　Resig-nated to my lot—
　　Which putts me in mind o' what
　　　'S called "The Literary."

Us folks in the country sees
　　Lots o' fun!—Take spellin'-school;
Er ole hoe-down jamborees;
　　Er revivals; er ef you'll

Tackle taffy-pullin's you
Kin git fun, and quite a few!—
  Same with huskin's. But all these
Kind o' frolics they hain't new
By a hunderd year' er two,
  Cipher on it as you please!
But I'll tell you what I jest
Think walks over all the rest—
Anyway it suits *me* best,—
    That's "The Literary."

First they started it—" 'y gee!"
  Thinks-says-I, "this settle-ment
'S gittin' too high-toned fer me!"
    But when all begin to jine,
    And I heerd *Izory* went,
    I jest kind o' drapped in line,
Like you've seen some sandy, thin,
  Scrawny shoat putt fer the crick
  Down some pig-trail through the thick
Spice-bresh, where the whole drove's been
'Bout six weeks 'fore he gits in!—
"Can't tell nothin'," I-says-ee,
" 'Bout it tel you go and see
    Their blame 'Literary'!"

Very first night I was there
   I was 'p'inted to be what
They call "Critic"—so's a fair
   And square jedgment could be got
    On the pieces 'at was read,
And on the debate,—"Which air
   Most destructive element,
    Fire er worter?" Then they hed
   Compositions on "Content,"
"Death," and "Botany"; and Tomps
He read one on "Dreenin' Swamps"
I p'nounced the boss, and said,
"*So* fur, 'at's the best thing read
    In yer 'Literary'!"

Then they *sung* some—tel I called
   Order, and got back ag'in
In the critic's cheer, and hauled
   All o' the p'formers in:—
Mandy Brizendine read one
   I fergit; and Doc's was "Thought";
And Sarepty's, hern was "None
   Air Denied 'at Knocks"; and Daut—
Fayette Strawnse's little niece—
She got up and spoke a piece:

Then Izory she read hern—
"Best thing in the whole concern,"
I-says-ee; "now le' 's adjourn
    This-here 'Literary'!"

They was some contendin'—yit
    We broke up in harmony.
Road outside as white as grit,
    And as slick as slick could be!—
I'd fetched 'Zory in my sleigh,—
And I had a heap to say,
    Drivin' back—in fact, I driv
'Way around the old north way,
    Where the Daubenspeckses live.
'Zory allus—'fore that night—
Never 'peared to feel jest right
In my company.—You see,
On'y thing on earth saved me
    Was that "Literary"!

DOWN TO THE CAPITAL

I' BE'N down to the Capital at Washington, D. C.,
    Where Congerss meets and passes on the pensions ort
        to be
Allowed to old one-legged chaps, like me, 'at sence the
    war
Don't wear their pants in pairs at all—and yit how proud
    we are!

Old Flukens, from our deestrick, jes' turned in and tuck
    and made
Me stay with him whilse I was there; and longer 'at I
    stayed
The more I kep' a-wantin' jes' to kind o' git away,
And yit a-feelin' sociabler with Flukens ever' day.

You see I'd got the idy—and I guess most folks agrees—
'At men as rich as him, you know, kin do jes' what they
    please;
A man worth stacks o' money, and a Congerssman and
    all,
And livin' in a buildin' bigger'n Masonic Hall!

Now mind, I'm not a-faultin' Fluke—he made his
    money square:
We both was Forty-niners, and both bu'sted gittin' there;
I weakened and onwindlassed, and he stuck and stayed
    and made
His millions; don't know what *I'm* worth untel my pen-
    sion's paid.

But I was goin' to tell you—er a-ruther goin' to try
To tell you how he's livin' now: gas burnin' mighty nigh
In ever' room about the house; and ever' night about,
Some blame reception goin' on, and money goin' out.

They's people there from all the world—jes' ever' kind
    'at lives,
Injuns and all! and Senaters, and Ripresentatives;
And girls, you know, jes' dressed in gauze and roses I
    *de*clare,
And even old men shamblin' round and a-waltzin' with
    'em there!

And bands a-tootin' circus-tunes, 'way in some other room
Jes' chokin' full o' hothouse plants and pinies and per-
    fume;
And fountains, squirtin' stiddy all the time; and statutes,
    made
Out o' puore marble, 'peared-like, sneakin' round there
    in the shade.

And Fluke he coaxed and begged and pled with *me* to
 take a hand
And sashay in amongst 'em—crutch and all, you under-
 stand;
But when I said how tired I was, and made fer open air,
He follered, and tel five o'clock we set a-talkin' there.

"My God!" says he—Fluke says to me, "I'm tireder'n
 you;
Don't putt up yer tobacker tel you give a man a chew.
Set back a leetle furder in the shadder—that'll do;
I'm tireder'n you, old man; I'm tireder'n you.

"You see that-air old dome," says he, "humped up ag'inst
 the sky?
It's grand, first time you see it; but it changes, by and by,
And then it stays jes' thataway—jes' anchored high and
 dry
Betwixt the sky up yender and the achin' of yer eye.

"Night's purty; not so purty, though, as what it ust to be
When my first wife was livin'. You remember her?"
 says he.
I nodded-like, and Fluke went on, "I wonder now ef she
Knows where I am—and what I am—and what I ust to
 be?

"That band in there!—I ust to think 'at music couldn't
   wear
A feller out the way it does; but that ain't music there—
That's jes' a' *imitation*, and like ever'thing, I swear,
I hear, er see, er tetch, er taste, er tackle anywhere!

"It's all jes' *artificial*, this-'ere high-priced life of ours;
The theory, *it's* sweet enough, tel it saps down and sours.
They's no *home* left, ner *ties* o' home about it.   By the
   powers,
The whole thing's artificialer'n artificial flowers!

"And all I want, and could lay down and *sob* fer, is to
   know
The homely things of homely life; fer instance, jes' to go
And set down by the kitchen stove—Lord! that 'u'd rest
   me so,—
Jes' set there, like I ust to do, and laugh and joke, you
   know.

"Jes' set there, like I ust to do," says Fluke, a-startin' in,
'Peared-like, to say the whole thing over to hisse'f ag'in;
Then stopped and turned, and kind o' coughed, and
   stooped and fumbled fer
Somepin' o' 'nuther in the grass—I guess his handker-
   cher.

Well, sence I'm back from Washington, where I left
    Fluke a-still
A-leggin' fer me, heart and soul, on that-air pension bill,
I've half-way struck the notion, when I think o' wealth
    and sich,
They's nothin' much patheticker'n jes' a-bein' rich!

THE OLD MAN AND JIM

OLD man never had much to say—
   'Ceptin' to Jim,—
     And Jim was the wildest boy he had—
  And the old man jes' wrapped up in him!
Never heerd him speak but once
   Er twice in my life,—and first time was
     When the army broke out, and Jim he went,
The old man backin' him, fer three months;
And all 'at I heerd the old man say
Was, jes' as we turned to start away,—
   "Well, good-by, Jim:
     Take keer of yourse'f!"

'Peared-like, he was more satisfied
   Jes' *lookin'* at Jim
And likin' him all to hisse'f-like, see?—
   'Cause he was jes' wrapped up in him!
And over and over I mind the day
The old man come and stood round in the way
   While we was drillin', a-watchin' Jim—
And down at the deepo a-heerin' him say,

"Well, good-by, Jim:
   Take keer of yourse'f!"

Never was nothin' about the *farm*
   Disting'ished Jim;
Neighbors all ust to wonder why
   The old man 'peared wrapped up in him:
But when Cap. Biggler he writ back
   'At Jim was the bravest boy we had
In the whole dern rigiment, white er black,
   And his fightin' good as his farmin' bad—
'At he had led, with a bullet clean
      Bored through his thigh, and carried the flag
Through the bloodiest battle you ever seen,—
The old man wound up a letter to him
'At Cap. read to us, 'at said : "Tell Jim
   Good-by,
      And take keer of hisse'f."

Jim come home jes' long enough
   To take the whim
'At he'd like to go back in the calvery—
   And the old man jes' wrapped up in him!
Jim 'lowed 'at he'd had sich luck afore,
Guessed he'd tackle her three years more.
And the old man give him a colt he'd raised,
And follered him over to Camp Ben Wade,

And laid around fer a week er so,
Watchin' Jim on dress-parade—
Tel finally he rid away,
And last he heerd was the old man say,—
    "Well, good-by, Jim:
        Take keer of yourse'f!"

Tuk the papers, the old man did,
    A-watchin' fer Jim—
Fully believin' he'd make his mark
    Some way—jes' wrapped up in him!—
And many a time the word 'u'd come
'At stirred him up like the tap of a drum—
At Petersburg, fer instunce, where
Jim rid right into their cannons there,
And *tuk* 'em, and p'inted 'em t'other way,
And socked it home to the boys in gray
    As they scooted fer timber, and on and on—
    Jim a lieutenant, and one arm gone,
And the old man's words in his mind all day,—
    "Well, good-by, Jim:
        Take keer of yourse'f!"

Think of a private, now, perhaps,
    We'll say like Jim,
'At's clumb clean up to the shoulder-straps—
    And the old man jes' wrapped up in him!

Think of him—with the war plum' through,
And the glorious old Red-White-and-Blue
A-laughin' the news down over Jim,
And the old man, bendin' over him—
The surgeon turnin' away with tears
'At hadn't leaked fer years and years,
As the hand of the dyin' boy clung to
His father's, the old voice in his ears,—
  "Well, good-by, Jim:
    Take keer of yourse'f!"

HERR WEISER

HERR WEISER!—Threescore-years-and-
    ten,—
    A hale white rose of his countrymen,
Transplanted here in the Hoosier loam,
And blossomy as his German home—
As blossomy and as pure and sweet
As the cool green glen of his calm retreat,
Far withdrawn from the noisy town
Where trade goes clamoring up and down,
Whose fret and fever, and stress and strife,
May not trouble his tranquil life!

Breath of rest, what a balmy gust!—
Quit of the city's heat and dust,
Jostling down by the winding road,
Through the orchard ways of his quaint abode.—
Tether the horse, as we onward fare
Under the pear-trees trailing there,
And thumping the wooden bridge at night
With lumps of ripeness and lush delight,

Till the stream, as it maunders on till dawn,
Is powdered and pelted and smiled upon.

Herr Weiser, with his wholesome face,
And the gentle blue of his eyes, and grace
Of unassuming honesty,
Be there to welcome you and me!
And what though the toil of the farm be stopped
And the tireless plans of the place be dropped,
While the prayerful master's knees are set
In beds of pansy and mignonette
And lily and aster and columbine,
Offered in love, as yours and mine?—

What, but a blessing of kindly thought,
Sweet as the breath of forget-me-not!—
What, but a spirit of lustrous love
White as the aster he bends above!—
What, but an odorous memory
Of the dear old man, made known to me
In days demanding a help like his,—
As sweet as the life of the lily is—
As sweet as the soul of a babe, bloom-wise
Born of a lily in paradise.

MARTHY ELLEN

THEY'S nothin' in the name to strike
    A feller more'n common like!
    'Taint liable to git no praise
Ner nothin' like it nowadays;
An' yit that name o' her'n is jest
As purty as the purtiest—
And more'n that, I'm here to say
I'll live a-thinkin' thataway
        And die fer Marthy Ellen!

It may be I was prejudust
In favor of it from the fust—
'Cause I kin ricollect jest how
We met, and hear her mother now
A-callin' of her down the road—
And, aggervatin' little toad!—
I see her now, jest sort o' half-
Way disapp'inted, turn and laugh
        And mock her—"Marthy Ellen!"

Our people never had no fuss,
And yit they never tuck to us;
We neighbered back and foreds some;
Until they see she liked to come
To our house—and me and her
Was jest together ever'whur
And all the time—and when they'd see
That I liked her and she liked me,
              They'd holler "Marthy Ellen!"

When we growed up, and they shet down
On me and her a-runnin' roun'
Together, and her father said
He'd never leave her nary red,
So he'p him, ef she married me,
And so on—and her mother she
Jest agged the gyrl, and said she 'lowed
She'd ruther see her in her shroud,
              I *writ* to Marthy Ellen—

That is, I kind o' tuck my pen
In hand, and stated whur and when
The undersigned would be that night,
With two good hosses, saddled right
Fer lively travelin', in case
Her folks 'ud like to jine the race.

She sent the same note back, and writ
"The rose is red!" right under it—
          "Your'n allus, Marthy Ellen."

That's all, I reckon—Nothin' more
To tell but what you've heerd afore—
The same old story, sweeter though
Fer all the trouble, don't you know.
Old-fashioned name! and yit it's jest
As purty as the purtiest;
And more'n that, I'm here to say
I'll live a-thinkin' thataway,
          And die fer Marthy Ellen!

AN OLD MAN'S MEMORY

THE delights of our childhood is soon passed
        away,
      And our gloryus youth it departs,—
And yit, dead and burried, they's blossoms of **May**
    Ore theyr medderland graves in our harts.
So, friends of my barefooted days on the farm,
    Whether truant in city er not,
God prosper you same as He's prosperin' me,
    Whilse your past hain't despised er forgot.

Oh! they's nothin', at morn, that's as grand unto me
    As the glorys of Natchur so fare,—
With the Spring in the breeze, and the bloom in the trees,
    And the hum of the bees ev'rywhare!
The green in the woods, and the birds in the boughs,
    And the dew spangled over the fields;
And the bah of the sheep and the bawl of the cows
    And the call from the house to your meals!

Then ho! fer your brekfast! and ho! fer the toil
That waiteth alike man and beast!
Oh! it's soon with my team I'll be turnin' up soil,
Whilse the sun shoulders up in the East
Ore the tops of the ellums and beeches and oaks,
To smile his Godspeed on the plow,
And the furry and seed, and the Man in his need,
And the joy of the swet of his brow!

WORTERMELON TIME

OLD wortermelon time is a-comin' round ag'in,
    And they ain't no man a-livin' any tickleder'n
        me,
Fer the way I hanker after wortermelons is a sin—
    Which is the why and wharefore, as you can plainly
        see.

Oh! it's in the sandy soil wortermelons does the best,
    And it's thare they'll lay and waller in the sunshine
        and the dew
Tel they wear all the green streaks clean off of theyr
        breast;
    And you bet I ain't a-findin' any fault with them; air
        you?

They ain't no better thing in the vegetable line;
    And they don't need much 'tendin', as ev'ry farmer
        knows;
And when theyr ripe and ready fer to pluck from the
        vine,
    I want to say to you theyr the best fruit that grows.

It's some likes the yeller-core, and some likes the red,
　　And it's some says "The Little Californy" is the best;
But the sweetest slice of all I ever wedged in my head,
　　Is the old "Edingburg Mounting-sprout," of the West.

You don't want no punkins nigh your wortermelon
　　　　vines—
　　'Cause, some-way-another, they'll spile your melons,
　　　　shore;—
I've seed 'em taste like punkins, from the core to the
　　　　rines,
　　Which may be a fact you have heerd of before.

But your melons that's raised right and 'tended to with
　　　　care,
　　You can walk around amongst 'em with a parent's
　　　　pride and joy,
And thump 'em on the heads with as fatherly a air
　　As ef each one of them was your little girl er boy.

I joy in my hart jest to hear that rippin' sound
　　When you split one down the back and jolt the halves
　　　　in two,
And the friends you love the best is gethered all around—
　　And you says unto your sweethart, "Oh, here's the
　　　　core fer you!"

And I like to slice 'em up in big pieces fer 'em all,
  Espeshally the childern, and watch theyr high delight
As one by one the rines with theyr pink notches falls,
  And they holler fer some more, with unquenched ap-
    petite.

Boys takes to it natchurl, and I like to see 'em eat—
  A slice of wortermelon's like a frenchharp in theyr
    hands,
And when they "saw" it through theyr mouth sich music
    can't be beat—
  'Cause it's music both the sperit and the stummick
    understands.

Oh, they's more in wortermelons than the purty-colored
    meat,
  And the overflowin' sweetness of the worter squshed
    betwixt
The up'ard and the down'ard motions of a feller's teeth,
  And it's the taste of ripe old age and juicy childhood
    mixed.

Fer I never taste a melon but my thoughts flies away
  To the summertime of youth; and again I see the
    dawn,
And the fadin' afternoon of the long summer day,
  And the dusk and dew a-fallin', and the night
    a-comin' on.

And thare's the corn around us, and the lispin' leaves and
    trees,
  And the stars a-peekin' down on us as still as silver
      mice,
And us boys in the wortermelons on our hands and knees,
  And the new-moon hangin' ore us like a yeller-cored
      slice.

Oh! it's wortermelon time is a-comin' round ag'in,
  And they ain't no man a-livin' any tickleder'n me,
Fer the way I hanker after wortermelons is a sin—
  Which is the why and wharefore, as you can plainly
      see.

WHEN THE FROST IS ON THE PUNKIN

WHEN the frost is on the punkin and the
    fodder's in the shock,
    And you hear the kyouck and gobble of the
struttin' turkey-cock,
And the clackin' of the guineys, and cluckin' of the hens,
And the rooster's hallylooer as he tiptoes on the fence;
O, it's then's the times a feller is a-feelin' at his best,
With the risin' sun to greet him from a night of peaceful
    rest,
As he leaves the house, bare-headed, and goes out to feed
    the stock,
When the frost is on the punkin and the fodder's in the
    shock.

They's something kindo' harty-like about the atmusfere
When the heat of summer's over and the coolin' fall is
    here—
Of course we miss the flowers, and the blossums on the
    trees,
And the mumble of the hummin'-birds and the buzzin'
    of the bees;

But the air's so appetizin'; and the landscape through the
    haze
Of a crisp and sunny morning of the airly autumn days
Is a pictur' that no painter has the colorin' to mock—
When the frost is on the punkin and the fodder's in the
    shock

The husky, rusty russel of the tossels of the corn,
And the raspin' of the tangled leaves, as golden as the
    morn;
The stubble in the furries—kindo' lonesome-like, but
    still
A-preachin' sermuns to us of the barns they growed to
    fill;
The strawstack in the medder, and the reaper in the shed;
The hosses in theyr stalls below—the clover overhead!—
O, it sets my hart a-clickin' like the tickin' of a clock,
When the frost is on the punkin and the fodder's in the
    shock!

Then your apples all is getherd, and the ones a feller
    keeps
Is poured around the celler-floor in red and yeller heaps;
And your cider-makin' 's over, and your wimmern-folks
    is through
With their mince and apple-butter, and theyr souse and
    saussage, too! . . .

I don't know how to tell it—but ef sich a thing could be
As the Angels wantin' boardin', and they'd call around
      on *me*—
I'd want to 'commodate 'em—all the whole-indurin'
      flock—
When the frost is on the punkin and the fodder's in the
      shock!

AUGUST

A DAY of torpor in the sullen heat
 Of Summer's passion: In the sluggish stream
 The panting cattle lave their lazy feet,
With drowsy eyes, and dream.

Long since the winds have died, and in the sky
 There lives no cloud to hint of Nature's grief;
The sun glares ever like an evil eye,
 And withers flower and leaf.

Upon the gleaming harvest-field remote
 The thresher lies deserted, like some old
Dismantled galleon that hangs afloat
 Upon a sea of gold.

The yearning cry of some bewildered bird.
 Above an empty nest, and truant boys
Along the river's shady margin heard—
 A harmony of noise—

A melody of wrangling voices blent
  With liquid laughter, and with rippling calls
Of piping lips and trilling echoes sent
  To mimic waterfalls.

And through the hazy veil the atmosphere
  Has draped about the gleaming face of Day,
The sifted glances of the sun appear
  In splinterings of spray.

The dusty highway, like a cloud of dawn,
  Trails o'er the hillside, and the passer-by,
A tired ghost in misty shroud, toils on
  His journey to the sky.

And down across the valley's drooping sweep,
  Withdrawn to farthest limit of the glade,
The forest stands in silence, drinking deep
  Its purple wine of shade.

The gossamer floats up on phantom wing;
  The sailor-vision voyages the skies
And carries into chaos everything
  That freights the weary eyes:

Till, throbbing on and on, the pulse of heat
  Increases—reaches—passes fever's height,
And Day sinks into slumber, cool and sweet,
  Within the arms of Night.

BACK FROM TOWN

OLD friends allus is the best,
  Halest-like and heartiest:
  Knowed us first, and don't allow
We're so blame much better now!
They was standin' at the bars
When we grabbed "the kivvered kyars"
And lit out fer town, to make
Money—and that old mistake!

We thought then the world we went
Into beat "The Settlement,"
And the friends 'at we'd make there
Would beat any anywhere!—
And they *do*—fer that's their biz:
They beat all the friends they is—
'Cept the raal old friends like you
'At staid home, like *I'd* ort to!

W'y, of all the good things yit
I ain't shet of, is to quit

Business, and git back to sheer
These old comforts waitin' here—
These old friends; and these old hands
'At a feller understands;
These old winter nights, and old
Young-folks chased in out the cold!

Sing "Hard Times'll come ag'in
No More!" and neighbers all jine in!
Here's a feller come from town
Wants that-air old fiddle down
From the chimbly!—Git the floor
Cleared fer one cowtillion more!—
It's poke the kitchen fire, says he,
And shake a friendly leg with me!

A DREAM OF AUTUMN

MELLOW hazes, lowly trailing
  Over wood and meadow, veiling
  Somber skies, with wild-fowl sailing
Sailor-like to foreign lands;
And the north-wind overleaping
Summer's brink, and flood-like sweeping
Wrecks of roses where the weeping-
  Willows wring their helpless hands.

Flared, like Titan torches flinging
Flakes of flame and embers, springing
From the vale, the trees stand swinging
  In the moaning atmosphere;
While in dead'ning lands the lowing
Of the cattle, sadder growing,
Fills the sense to overflowing
  With the sorrow of the year.

Sorrowfully, yet the sweeter
Sings the brook in rippled meter
Under boughs that lithely teeter

Lorn birds, answering from the shores
Through the viny, shady-shiny
Interspaces, shot with tiny
Flying motes that fleck the winy
    Wave-engraven sycamores.

Fields of ragged stubble, wrangled
With rank weeds, and shocks of tangled
Corn, with crests like rent plumes dangled
    Over Harvest's battle-plain;
And the sudden whir and whistle
Of the quail that, like a missile,
Whizzes over thorn and thistle,
    And, a missile, drops again.

Muffled voices, hid in thickets
Where the redbird stops to stick its
Ruddy beak betwixt the pickets
    Of the truant's rustic trap;
And the sound of laughter ringing
Where, within the wild vine swinging,
Climb Bacchante's schoolmates, flinging
    Purple clusters in her lap.

Rich as wine, the sunset flashes
Round the tilted world, and dashes
Up the sloping west, and splashes
    Red foam over sky and sea—
Till my dream of Autumn, paling
In the splendor all-prevailing,
Like a sallow leaf goes sailing
    Down the silence solemnly.

THE BOYS

WHERE are they?—the friends of my child-
hood enchanted—
The clear, laughing eyes looking back in
my own,
And the warm, chubby fingers my palms have so wanted,
As when we raced over
Pink pastures of clover,
And mocked the quail's whir and the bumblebee's
drone?

Have the breezes of time blown their blossomy faces
Forever adrift down the years that are flown?
Am I never to see them romp back to their places,
Where over the meadow,
In sunshine and shadow,
The meadow-larks trill, and the bumblebees drone?

Where are they? Ah! dim in the dust lies the clover;
The whippoorwill's call has a sorrowful tone,
And the dove's—I have wept at it over and over;—
I want the glad lustre
Of youth, and the cluster
Of faces asleep where the bumblebees drone!

THE FIRST BLUEBIRD

JEST rain and snow! and rain again!
   And dribble! drip! and blow!
    Then snow! and thaw! and slush! and then—
  Some more rain and snow!

This morning I was 'most afeard
   To *wake* up—when, I jing!
I seen the sun shine out and heerd
   The first bluebird of Spring!—
Mother she'd raised the winder some;—
And in acrost the orchurd come,
   Soft as a' angel's wing,
A breezy, treesy, beesy hum,
   Too sweet fer anything!

The winter's shroud was rent apart—
   The sun bu'st forth in glee,—
And when *that bluebird* sung, my hart
   Hopped out o' bed with me!

TOWN AND COUNTRY

THEY'S a predjudice allus 'twixt country and
      town
    Which I wisht in my hart wasent so.
You take *city* people, jest square up and down,
    And they're mighty good people to know:
And whare's better people a-livin', to-day,
    Than us in the *country?* —Yit good
As both of us is, we're divorsed, you might say,
    And won't compermise when we could!

Now as nigh into town fer yer Pap, ef you please,
    Is what's called the sooburbs.—Fer thare
You'll at least ketch a whiff of the breeze and a sniff
    Of the breth of wild-flowrs ev'rywhare.
They's room fer the childern to play, and grow, too—
    And to roll in the grass, er to climb
Up a tree and rob nests, like they *ortent* to do,
    But they'll do *anyhow* ev'ry time!

254

My Son-in-law said, when he lived in the town,
    He jest natchurly pined, night and day,
Fer a sight of the woods, er a acre of ground
    Whare the trees wasent all cleared away!
And he says to me onc't, whilse a-visitin' us
    On the farm, "It's not strange, I declare,
That we can't coax you folks, without raisin' a fuss,
    To come to town, visitin' thare!"

And says I, "Then git back whare you sorto' *belong*—
    And *Madaline*, too,—and yer three
Little childern," says I, "that don't know a bird-song,
    Ner a hawk from a chicky-dee-dee!
Git back," I-says-I, "to the blue of the sky
    And the green of the fields, and the shine
Of the sun, with a laugh in yer voice and yer eye
    As harty as Mother's and mine!"

Well—long-and-short of it,—he's compermised *some*—
    He's moved in the sooburbs.—And now
They don't haf to coax, when they want us to come,
    'Cause we turn in and go *anyhow!*
Fer thare—well, they's room fer the songs and purfume
    Of the grove and the old orchurd-ground,
And they's room fer the childern out thare, and they's
        room
    Fer theyr Gran'pap to waller 'em round!

DECORATION DAY ON THE PLACE

IT'S lonesome—sorto' lonesome,—it's a *Sund'y-day*,
    to me,
    It 'pears-like—more'n any day I nearly ever see!—
Yit, with the Stars and Stripes above, a-flutterin' in the
    air,
On ev'ry Soldier's grave I'd love to lay a lily thare.

They say, though, Decoration Day is giner'ly observed
'Most *ev'rywhares*—espeshally by soldier-boys that's
    served.—
But me and Mother's never went—we seldom git
    away,—
In p'int o' fact, we're *allus* home on *Decoration Day*.

They say the old boys marches through the streets in
    colum's grand,
A-follerin' the old war-tunes they're playin' on the
    band—
And citizuns all jinin' in—and little childern, too—
All marchin', under shelter of the old Red White and
    Blue.—

With roses! roses! roses!—ev'rybody in the town!—
And crowds o' little girls in white, jest fairly loaded
      down!—
Oh! don't THE BOYS know it, from theyr camp acrost
      the hill? —
Don't they see theyr com'ards comin' and the old flag
      wavin' still?

Oh! can't they hear the bugul and the rattle of the
      drum?—
Ain't they no way under heavens they can rickollect us
      some?
Ain't they no way we can coax 'em, through the roses,
      jest to say
They know that ev'ry day on earth's theyr Decoration
      Day?

We've tried that—me and Mother,—whare Elias takes
      his rest,
In the orchurd—in his uniform, and hands acrost his
      brest,
And the flag he died fer, smilin' and a-ripplin' in the
      breeze
Above his grave—and over that,—*the robin in the trees!*

And *yit* it's lonesome—lonesome!—It's a *Sund'y-day,*
to *me,*
It 'pears-like—more'n any day I nearly ever see!—
Still, with the Stars and Stripes above, a-flutterin' in the
air,
On ev'ry Soldier's grave I'd love to lay a lily thare.

THE OLD BAND

IT'S mighty good to git back to the old town, shore,
  Considerin' I've be'n away twenty year and more.
  Sence I moved then to Kansas, of course I see a
    change,
A-comin' back, and notice things that's new to me and
    strange;
Especially at evening when yer new band-fellers meet,
In fancy uniforms and all, and play out on the street—
. . . What's come of old Bill Lindsey and the Saxhorn
    fellers—say?
        I want to hear the *old* band play.

What's come of Eastman, and Nat Snow? And where's
    War Barnett at?
And Nate and Bony Meek; Bill Hart; Tom Richa'son
    and that
Air brother of him played the drum as twic't as big as
    Jim;
And old Hi Kerns, the carpenter—say, what's become o'
    him?

259

I make no doubt yer *new band* now's a *competenter* band,
And plays their music more by note than what they play
    by hand,
And stylisher and grander tunes; but somehow—*any-*
    way,
        I want to hear the *old* band play.

Sich tunes as "John Brown's Body" and "Sweet Alice,"
    don't you know;
And "The Camels Is A-Comin'," and "John Anderson,
    My Jo";
And a dozent others of 'em—"Number Nine" and
    "Number 'Leven"
Was favo-*rites* that fairly made a feller dream o'
    Heaven.
And when the boys 'u'd saranade, I've laid so still in bed
I've even heerd the locus'-blossoms droppin' on the shed
When "Lily Dale," er "Hazel Dell," had sobbed and
    died away—
       . . . I want to hear the *old* band play.

Yer *new* band ma'by beats it, but the *old band*'s what I
    said—
It allus 'peared to kind o' chord with somepin' in my
    head;

And, whilse I'm no musicianer, when my blame' eyes is
    jes'
Nigh drownded out, and Mem'ry squares her jaws and
    sort o' says
She *won't* ner *never will* fergit, I want to jes' turn in
And take and light right out o' here and git back West
    ag'in
And *stay* there, when I git there, where I never haf' to
    say

        I want to hear the *old* band play.

"LAST CHRISTMAS WAS A YEAR AGO"

THE OLD LADY SPEAKS

LAST Christmas was a year ago,
　　Says I to David, I-says-I,
　　"We're goin' to morning service, so
　You hitch up right away: I'll try
To tell the girls jes' what to do
Fer dinner.—We'll be back by two."
I didn't wait to hear what he
Would more'n like say back to me,
But banged the stable door and flew
Back to the house, jes' plumb chilled through.

Cold! *Wooh!* how cold it was! My-oh!
Frost flyin', and the air, you know,
"Jes' sharp enough," heerd David swear,
"To shave a man and cut his hair!"
And blow and blow! and snow and snow!—
　Where it had drifted 'long the fence
And 'crost the road,—some places, though,
Jes' swep' clean to the gravel, so

The goin' was as bad fer sleighs
As 'twas fer wagons,—and both ways,
'Twixt snow-drifts and the bare ground, I've
Jes' wundered we got through alive;
    I hain't saw nothin', 'fore er sence,
'At beat it anywheres, I know—
Last Christmas was a year ago.

And David said, as we set out,
'At Christmas services was 'bout
    As cold and wuthless kind o' love
        To offer up as he knowed of;
And as fer him, he railly thought
    'At the Good Bein' up above
Would think more of us—as He ought—
A-stayin' home on sich a day,
And thankin' of Him thataway!
And jawed on, in an undertone,
'Bout leavin' Lide and Jane alone
There on the place, and me not there
To oversee 'em, and p'pare
The stuffin' fer the turkey, and
The sass and all, you understand.

I've allus managed David by
Jes' sayin' *nothin'*. That was why
He'd chased Lide's beau away—'cause Lide
She'd allus take up Perry's side
When David tackled him; and so,
Last Christmas was a year ago,—
Er ruther, 'bout *a week afore,*—
  David and Perry'd quarr'l'd about
Some tom-fool argyment, you know,
  And Pap told him to "Jes' git out
O' there, and not to come no more,
And, when he went, to shet the door!"
And as he passed the winder, we
Saw Perry, white as white could be,
March past, onhitch his hoss, and light
A see-gyar, and lope out o' sight.
Then Lide she come to me and cried!
  And I said nothin'—was no need.
And yit, you know, that man jes' got
Right out o' there's ef he'd be'n shot,
  P'tendin' he must go and feed
The stock er somepin'. Then I tried
To git the pore girl pacified.

But, gittin' back to—where was we?—
Oh, yes!—where David lectered me
All way to meetin', high and low,
Last Christmas was a year ago:
Fer all the awful cold, they was
A fair attendunce; mostly, though,
The crowd was 'round the stoves, you see,
Thawin' their heels and scrougin' us.

Ef 't 'adn't be'n fer the old Squire
Givin' *his* seat to us, as in
We stomped, a-fairly perishin',
    And David could 'a' got no fire,
He'd jes' 'a' drapped there in his tracks:
    And Squire, as I was tryin' to yit
Make room fer him, says, "No; the fac's
    Is, *I* got to git up and git
'Ithout no preachin'. Jes' got word—
Trial fer life—can't be deferred!"
And out he putt!

. . . . . . And all way through
The sermont—and a long one, too—
I couldn't he'p but think o' Squire
And us changed round so, and admire
His gintle ways,—to give his warm
Bench up, and have to face the storm.
And when I noticed David he

Was needin' jabbin'—I thought best
　　To kind o' sort o' let him rest:
'Peared-like he slep' so peacefully!
And then I thought o' home, and how
And what the gyrls was doin' now,
　　And kind o' prayed, 'way in my breast,
And breshed away a tear er two
As David waked, and church was through.

By time we'd "howdyed" round and shuck
Hands with neighbors, must 'a' tuck
A half hour longer: ever' one
　　A-sayin' "Christmas gift!" afore
David er me—so we got none!
　　But David warmed up, more and more,
And got so jokey-like, and had
His sperits up, and 'peared so glad,
　　I whispered to him, "S'pose you ast
　　　A passel of 'em come and eat
Their dinners with us. Gyrls's got
A full-and-plenty fer the lot
　　And all their kin!" So David passed
　　　The invite round: and ever' seat
In ever' wagon-bed and sleigh
Was jes' packed, as we rode away,—
The young folks, mil'd er so along,
A-strikin' up a sleighin'-song,

Tel David laughed and yelled, you know,
And jes' whirped up and sent the snow
  And gravel flyin' thick and fast—
Last Christmas was a year ago.
W'y, that-air seven-mil'd ja'nt we come—
Jes' seven mil'd scant from church to home—
It didn't 'pear, *that* day, to be
Much furder railly 'n 'bout *three!*

But I was purty squeamish by
The time home hove in sight and I
See two vehickles standin' there
Already.   So says I, *"Prepare!"*
All to myse'f.   And presently
David he sobered; and says he,
  "Hain't that-air Squire Hanch's old
Buggy," he says, "and claybank mare?"
  Says I, "Le' 's git in out the cold—
    Your company's nigh 'bout froze!" He says,
"Whose sleigh's that-air, a-standin' there?"
    Says I, "It's no odds *whose—you* jes'
Drive to the house and let us out,
'Cause we're jes' *freezin'*, nigh about!"
  Well, David swung up to the door,
And out we piled.   And first I heerd
  Jane's voice, then *Lide's*,—I thought afore
  I reached that gyrl I'd jes' die, shore;

267

And *when* I reached her, wouldn't keered
    Much ef I had, I was so glad,
A-kissin' her through my green veil,
    And jes' excitin' her so bad,
        'At *she* broke down *herse'f*—and Jane,
        She cried—and we all hugged again.
And *David?*—David jes' turned pale!—
    Looked at the gyrls, and then at me,
Then at the open door—and then—
    "Is old Squire Hanch in there?" says he.
The old Squire suddenly stood in
The doorway, with a sneakin' grin.
"Is Perry Anders in there, too?"
Says David, limberin' all through,
As Lide and me both grabbed him, and
Perry stepped out and waved his hand
And says, "Yes, Pap." And David jes'
Stooped and kissed Lide, and says, "I guess
Yer *mother's* much to blame as you.
Ef *she* kin resk him, I kin too!"
    The dinner we had then hain't no
Bit better'n the one to-day
'At we'll have fer 'em. Hear some sleigh
A-jinglin' now. David, fer *me*,
I wish you'd jes' go out and see
Ef they're in sight yit. It jes' does

Me good to think, in times like these,
Lide's done so well.   And David, he's
More tractabler'n what he was—
Last Christmas was a year ago.

FESSLER'S BEES

"Talkin' 'bout yer bees," says Ike,
    Speakin' slow and ser'ous-like,
        "D' ever tell you 'bout old 'Bee'—
Old 'Bee' Fessler?" Ike says-he!
"Might call him a *bee-expert*,
    When it come to handlin' bees,—
Roll the sleeves up of his shirt
    And wade in amongst the trees
        Where a swarm 'u'd settle, and—
Blam'est man on top of dirt!
        Rake 'em with his naked hand
Right back in the hive ag'in,
    Jes' as easy as you please!
    Nary bee 'at split the breeze
Ever jabbed a stinger in
Old 'Bee' Fessler—jes' in fun,
Er in *airnest*—nary one!—
Couldn't agg one *on* to, nuther,
Ary one way er the other!

"Old 'Bee' Fessler," Ike says-he,
"Made a speshyality
Jes' o' bees; and built a shed—
    Len'th about a half a mild!
Had about a *thousan'* head
    O' hives, I reckon—tame and wild!
Durndest buzzin' ever wuz—
Wuss'n telegraph-poles does
When they're sockin' home the news
Tight as they kin let 'er loose!
Visitors rag out and come
Clean from town to hear 'em hum,
And stop at the kivered bridge;
But wuz some 'u'd cross the ridge
Allus, and go clos'ter—so's
They could *see* 'em hum, I s'pose!
'Peared-like strangers down that track
Allus met folks comin' back
Lookin' extry fat and hearty
Fer a city picnic party!

" 'Fore he went to Floridy,
Old 'Bee' Fessler," Ike says-he—
"Old 'Bee' Fessler couldn't bide
    Childern on his place," says Ike.
"Yit, fer all, they'd climb inside
    And tromp round there, keerless-like,

In their bare feet. 'Bee' could tell
Ev'ry town-boy by his yell—
So's 'at when they bounced the fence,
Didn't make no difference!
He'd jes' git down on one knee
In the grass and pat the bee!—
And, ef 't 'adn't stayed stuck in,
Fess' 'u'd set the sting ag'in,
'N' potter off, and wait around
Fer the old famillyer sound.
Allus boys there, more or less,
Scootin' round the premises!
When the buckwheat wuz in bloom,
Lawzy! how them bees 'u'd boom
Round the boys 'at crossed that way
Fer the crick on Saturday!
Never seemed to me su'prisin'
'At the sting o' bees 'uz p'izin!

" 'Fore he went to Floridy,"
Ike says, "nothin' 'bout a bee
  'At old Fessler didn't know,—
W'y, it jes' 'peared-like 'at he
  Knowed their language, high and low:
Claimed he told jes' by their buzz
What their wants and wishes wuz!

272

Peek in them-air little holes
    Round the porches o' the hive—
Drat their pesky little souls!—
    Could 'a' skinned the man alive!
Bore right in there with his thumb,
And squat down and scrape the gum
Outen ev'ry hole, and blow
'N' bresh the crumbs off, don't you know!
Take the roof off, and slide back
Them-air glass concerns they pack
Full o' honey, and jes' lean
'N' grabble 'mongst 'em fer the queen!
Fetch her out and *show* you to her—
Jes', you might say, *interview* her!

"Year er two," says Ike, says-he,
" 'Fore he went to Floridy,
Fessler struck the theory,
    Honey was the same as *love*—
      You could make it day and night:
Said them bees o' his could be
    Got jes' twic't the work out of
      Ef a feller managed right.
He contended ef bees found
Blossoms all the year around,
He could git 'em down at once
To work all the *winter* months

Same as *summer*. So, one fall,
    When their summer's work wuz done,
'Bee' turns in and robs 'em all;
    Loads the hives then, one by one,
On the cyars, and 'lowed he'd see
Ef bees loafed in *Floridy!*
Said he bet he'd know the reason
Ef *his* didn't work that season!

"And," says Ike, "it's jes'," says-he,
"Like old Fessler says to me:
'Any man kin fool a *bee*,
Git him down in Floridy!'
'Peared at fust, as old 'Bee' said,
Fer to kind o' turn their head
Fer a spell; but, bless you! they
Didn't lose a half a day
    Altogether!—Jes' lit in
        Them-air tropics, and them-air
    Cacktusses a-ripen-nin',
'N' magnolyers, and sweet-peas,
'N' 'simmon and pineapple trees,
    'N' ripe bananers, here and there,
'N' dates a-danglin' in the breeze,
    'N' figs and reezins ev'rywhere,
All waitin' jes' fer Fessler's bees!
'N' Fessler's bees, with gaumy wings,
A-gittin' down and *whoopin'* things!—

Fessler kind o' overseein'
'Em, and sort o' *'hee-o-heein'!'

" 'Fore he went to *Floridy*,
Old 'Bee' Fessler," Ike says-he,
"Wuzn't counted, jes' to say,
Mean er or'n'ry anyway;
On'y ev'ry 'tarnel dime
   'At 'u'd pass him on the road
He'd ketch up with, ev'ry time;
   And no mortal ever knowed
Him to spend a copper cent—
'Less on some fool-*'speriment*
With them *bees*—like that-un he
Played on 'em in Floridy.
Fess', of course, *he* tuck his ease,
But 'twuz *bilious* on the bees!
Sweat, you know, 'u'd jes' stand out
   On their *forreds*—pant and groan,
And grunt round and limp about!—
   And old 'Bee,' o' course, a-knowin'
'Twuzn't no fair shake to play
   On them pore dumb insecks, ner
To abuse 'em thataway.
Bees has rights, I'm here to say,
   And that's all they ast him fer!

Man as mean as *that*, jes' 'pears,
Could 'a' worked bees on the sheers!
Cleared big money—well, I guess,
'Bee' shipped honey, more er less,
Into ev'ry state, perhaps,
Ever putt down in the maps!

"But by time he fetched 'em back
   In the spring ag'in," says Ike,
   "They wuz actin' s'picious-like:
Though they 'peared to lost the track
   O' ev'rything they saw er heard,
      They'd lay round the porch, and gap'
At their shadders in the sun,
   Do-less like, ontel some bird
      Suddenly 'u'd maybe drap
In a bloomin' churry tree,
Twitterin' a tune 'at run
   In their minds familiously!
They'd revive up, kind o', then,
Like they argied: 'Well, it's be'n
The most longest summer we
Ever saw er want to see!
Must be *right*, though, er old "*Bee*"
'U'd notify us!' they says-ee;

And they'd sort o' square their chin
And git down to work ag'in—
Moanin' round their honey-makin',
Kind o' like their head was achin'.
Tetchin' fer to see how they
Trusted Fessler thataway—
Him a-lazin' round, and smirkin'
To hisse'f to see 'em workin'!

"But old 'Bee,'" says Ike, says-he,—
    "*Now* where is he?   *Where's* he gone?
Where's the head he helt so free?
Where's his pride and vanity?
    What's his hopes a-restin' on?—
Never knowed a man," says Ike,
    "Take advantage of a bee,
'At affliction didn't strike
    Round in that vicinity!
Sinners allus suffers some,
And *old Fessler's* reck'nin' come!
That-air man to-day is jes'
Like the grass 'at Scriptur' says
Cometh up, and then turns in
And jes' gits cut down ag'in!

Old 'Bee' Fessler," Ike says-he,
"Says, last fall, says he to me—
'Ike,' says he, 'them bees has jes'
Ciphered out my or'n'riness!
Nary bee in ary swarm
On the whole endurin' farm
Won't have nothin' more to do
  With a man as mean as I've
Be'n to them, last year er two!
  Nary bee in ary hive
But'll turn his face away,
Like they ort, whenever they
Hear my footprints drawin' nigh!'
And old 'Bee,' he'd sort o' shy
  Round oneasy in his cheer,
Wipe his eyes, and yit the sap,
Spite o' all, 'u'd haf' to drap,
  As he wound up: 'Wouldn't keer
Quite so much ef they'd jes' light
In and settle things up right,
Like they ort; but—blame the thing!—
'Pears-like they won't even *sting!*
Pepper me, the way I felt,
And I'd thank 'em, ev'ry welt!'

And as miz'able and mean
As 'Bee' looked, ef you'd 'a' seen
Them-air hungry eyes," says Ike,
"You'd fergive him, more'n like.

"Wisht you had 'a' knowed old 'Bee'
'Fore he went to Floridy!"

279

THE OLD TRUNDLE-BED

O THE old trundle-bed where I slept when a boy!
What canopied king might not covet the joy?
The glory and peace of that slumber of mine,
Like a long, gracious rest in the bosom divine:
The quaint, homely couch, hidden close from the light,
But daintily drawn from its hiding at night.
O a nest of delight, from the foot to the head,
Was the queer little, dear little, old trundle-bed!

O the old trundle-bed, where I wondering saw
The stars through the window, and listened with awe
To the sigh of the winds as they tremblingly crept
Through the trees where the robin so restlessly slept:
Where I heard the low, murmurous chirp of the wren,
And the katydid listlessly chirrup again,
Till my fancies grew faint and were drowsily led
Through the maze of the dreams of the old trundle-bed.

O the old trundle-bed! O the old trundle-bed!
With its plump little pillow, and old-fashioned spread;

Its snowy-white sheets, and the blankets above,
Smoothed down and tucked round with the touches of
        love;
The voice of my mother to lull me to sleep
With the old fairy stories my memories keep
Still fresh as the lilies that bloom o'er the head
Once bowed o'er my own in the old trundle-bed.

WHERE THE CHILDREN USED TO PLAY

THE old farm-home is Mother's yet and mine,
    And filled it is with plenty and to spare,—
    But we are lonely here in life's decline,
Though fortune smiles around us everywhere:
      We look across the gold
      Of the harvests, as of old—
The corn, the fragrant clover, and the hay;
      But most we turn our gaze,
      As with eyes of other days,
To the orchard where the children used to play.

O from our life's full measure
And rich hoard of worldly treasure
   We often turn our weary eyes away,
And hand in hand we wander
Down the old path winding yonder
   To the orchard where the children used to play.

Our sloping pasture-lands are filled with herds;
   The barn and granary-bins are bulging o'er;
The grove's a paradise of singing birds—
   The woodland brook leaps laughing by the door;
            Yet lonely, lonely still,
            Let us prosper as we will,
Our old hearts seem so empty everyway—
            We can only through a mist
            See the faces we have kissed
In the orchard where the children used to play.

O from our life's full measure
And rich hoard of worldly treasure
   We often turn our weary eyes away,
And hand in hand we wander
Down the old path winding yonder
   To the orchard where the children used to play.

THE HOSS

THE hoss he is a splendud beast;
　　He is man's friend, as heaven desined,
　　And, search the world from west to east,
No honester you'll ever find!

Some calls the hoss "a pore dumb brute,"
　　And yit, like Him who died fer you,
I say, as I theyr charge refute,
　　" 'Fergive; they know not what they do!' "

No wiser animal makes tracks
　　Upon these earthly shores, and hence
Arose the axium, true as facts,
　　Extoled by all, as "Good hoss-sense!"

The hoss is strong, and knows his stren'th,—
　　You hitch him up a time er two
And lash him, and he'll go his len'th
　　And kick the dashboard out fer you!

But, treat him allus good and kind,
    And never strike him with a stick,
Ner aggervate him, and you'll find
    He'll never do a hostile trick.

A hoss whose master tends him right
    And worters him with daily care,
Will do your biddin' with delight,
    And act as docile as *you* air.

He'll paw and prance to hear your praise,
    Because he's learnt to love you well;
And, though you can't tell what he says,
    He'll nicker all he wants to tell.

He knows you when you slam the gate
    At early dawn, upon your way
Unto the barn, and snorts elate,
    To git his corn, er oats, er hay.

He knows you, as the orphant knows
    The folks that loves her like theyr own,
And raises her and "finds" her clothes,
    And "schools" her tel a womern-grown!

I claim no hoss will harm a man,
  Ner kick, ner run away, cavort,
Stump-suck, er balk, er "catamaran,"
  Ef you'll jest treat him as you ort.

But when I see the beast abused,
  And clubbed around as I've saw some,
I want to see his owner noosed,
  And jest yanked up like Absolum!

Of course they's differunce in stock,—
  A hoss that has a little yeer,
And slender build, and shaller hock,
  Can beat his shadder, mighty near!

Whilse one that's thick in neck and chist
  And big in leg and full in flank,
That tries to race, I still insist
  He'll have to take the second rank.

And I have jest laid back and laughed,
  And rolled and wallered in the grass
At fairs, to see some heavy-draft
  Lead out at *first*, yit come in *last!*

Each hoss has his appinted place,—
    The heavy hoss should plow the soil;—
The blooded racer, he must race,
    And win big wages fer his toil.

I never bet—ner never wrought
    Upon my feller man to bet—
And yit, at times, I've often thought
    Of my convictions with regret.

I bless the hoss from hoof to head—
    From head to hoof, and tale to mane!—
I bless the hoss, as I have said,
    From head to hoof, and back again!

I love my God the first of all,
    Then Him that perished on the cross,
And next, my wife,—and then I fall
    Down on my knees and love the hoss.

OLD-FASHIONED ROSES

THEY ain't no style about 'em,
　　And they're sort o' pale and faded,
　　Yit the doorway here, without 'em,
Would be lonesomer, and shaded
　　With a good 'eal blacker shadder
　　　Than the morning-glories makes,
　　And the sunshine would look sadder
　　　Fer their good old-fashion' sakes.

I like 'em 'cause they kind o'
　　Sort o' *make* a feller like 'em!
And I tell you, when I find a
　　Bunch out whur the sun kin strike 'em,
　　　It allus sets me thinkin'
　　　　O' the ones 'at used to grow
　　　And peek in thro' the chinkin'
　　　　O' the cabin, don't you know!

And then I think o' mother,
 And how she ust to love 'em—
When they wuzn't any other,
 'Less she found 'em up above 'em!
  And her eyes, afore she shut 'em,
   Whispered with a smile and said
  We must pick a bunch and putt 'em
   In her hand when she wuz dead.

But, as I wuz a-sayin',
 They ain't no style about 'em
Very gaudy er displayin',
 But I wouldn't be without 'em—
  'Cause I'm happier in these posies,
   And the hollyhawks and sich,
  Than the hummin'-bird 'at noses
   In the roses of the rich.

GRIGGSBY'S STATION

PAP'S got his pattent-right, and rich as all creation;
But where's the peace and comfort that we all
had before?
Le's go a-visitin' back to Griggsby's Station—
Back where we ust to be so happy and so pore!

The likes of us a-livin' here!   It's jest a mortal pity
To see us in this great big house, with cyarpets on the
stairs,
And the pump right in the kitchen!   And the city! city!
city!—
And nothin' but the city all around us ever'wheres!

Climb clean above the roof and look from the steeple,
And never see a robin, nor a beech or ellum tree!
And right here in ear-shot of at least a thousan' people,
And none that neighbors with us or we want to go and
see!

Le's go a-visitin' back to Griggsby's Station—
  Back where the latch-string's a-hangin' from the
    door,
And ever' neighbor round the place is dear as a relation—
  Back where we ust to be so happy and so pore!

I want to see the Wiggenses, the whole kit-and-bilin',
  A-drivin' up from Shallor Ford to stay the Sunday
    through;
And I want to see 'em hitchin' at their son-in-law's
    and pilin'
  Out there at 'Lizy Ellen's like they ust to do!

I want to see the piece-quilts the Jones girls is makin';
  And I want to pester Laury 'bout their freckled hired
    hand,
And joke her 'bout the widower she come purt' nigh
    a-takin',
  Till her Pap got his pension 'lowed in time to save his
    land.

Le's go a-visitin' back to Griggsby's Station—
  Back where they's nothin' aggervatin' any more,
Shet away safe in the woods around the old location—
  Back where we ust to be so happy and so pore!

I want to see Marindy and he'p her with her sewin',
  And hear her talk so lovin' of her man that's dead and
    gone,
And stand up with Emanuel to show me how he's
    growin',
  And smile as I have saw her 'fore she putt her mourn-
    in' on.

And I want to see the Samples, on the old lower eighty,
  Where John, our oldest boy, he was tuk and burried—
    for
His own sake and Katy's,—and I want to cry with Katy
  As she reads all his letters over, writ from The War.

What's in all this grand life and high situation,
  And nary pink nor hollyhawk a-bloomin' at the
    door?—
Le's go a-visitin' back to Griggsby's Station—
  Back where we ust to be so happy and so pore!

KNEE-DEEP IN JUNE

I

TELL you what I like the best—
   'Long about knee-deep in June,
   'Bout the time strawberries melts
On the vine,—some afternoon
  Like to jes' git out and rest,
    And not work at nothin' else!

II

Orchard's where I'd ruther be—
Needn't fence it in fer me!—
  Jes' the whole sky overhead,
And the whole airth underneath—
Sort o' so's a man kin breathe
  Like he ort, and kind o' has
Elbow-room to keerlessly
   Sprawl out len'thways on the grass
    Where the shadders thick and soft
  As the kivvers on the bed
    Mother fixes in the loft
Allus, when they's company!

Jes' a-sort o' lazin' there—
  S'lazy, 'at you peek and peer
    Through the wavin' leaves above,
    Like a feller 'at's in love
And don't know it, ner don't keer!
Ever'thing you hear and see
    Got some sort o' interest—
    Maybe find a bluebird's nest
  Tucked up there conveenently
  Fer the boy 'at's ap' to be
  Up some other apple-tree!
Watch the swallers skootin' past
'Bout as peert as you could ast;
  Er the Bob-white raise and whiz
  Where some other's whistle is.

Ketch a shadder down below,
And look up to find the crow—
Er a hawk,—away up there,
'Pearantly *froze* in the air!
  Hear the old hen squawk, and squat
  Over ever' chick she's got,
Suddent-like!—and she knows where

That-air hawk is, well as you!—
You jes' bet yer life she do!—
    Eyes a-glitterin' like glass,
    Waitin' till he makes a pass!

V

Pee-wees' singin', to express
    My opinion, 's second class,
Yit you'll hear 'em more er less;
    Sapsucks gittin' down to biz,
Weedin' out the lonesomeness;
    Mr. Bluejay, full o' sass,
        In them base-ball clothes o' his,
Sportin' round the orchard jes'
Like he owned the premises!
    Sun out in the fields kin sizz,
But flat on yer back, I guess,
    In the shade's where glory is!
That's jes' what I'd like to do
Stiddy fer a year er two!

VI

Plague! ef they ain't somepin' in
Work 'at kind o' goes ag'in'

My convictions!—'long about
  Here in June especially!—
  Under some old apple-tree,
    Jes' a-restin' through and through
I could git along without
    Nothin' else at all to do
    Only jes' a-wishin' you
Wuz a-gittin' there like me,
And June was eternity!

VII

Lay out there and try to see
Jes' how lazy you kin be!—
  Tumble round and souse yer head
In the clover-bloom, er pull
    Yer straw hat acrost yer eyes
    And peek through it at the skies,
  Thinkin' of old chums 'at's dead,
      Maybe, smilin' back at you
In betwixt the beautiful
    Clouds o' gold and white and blue!—
Month a man kin railly love—
June, you know, I'm talkin' of!

VIII

March ain't never nothin' new!—
Aprile's altogether too
　　Brash fer me! and May—I jes'
　　'Bominate its promises,—
Little hints o' sunshine and
Green around the timber-land—
　　A few blossoms, and a few
　　Chip-birds, and a sprout er two,—
　　Drap asleep, and it turns in
　　'Fore daylight and *snows* ag'in!—
But when *June* comes—Clear my th'oat
　　With wild honey!—Rench my hair
In the dew! and hold my coat!
　　　　Whoop out loud! and th'ow my hat!—
June wants me, and I'm to spare!
Spread them shadders anywhere,
I'll git down and waller there,
　　　　And obleeged to you at that!

RABBIT

I S'POSE it takes a feller 'at's be'n
   Raised in a country-town, like me,
   To '*preciate* rabbits! . . . Eight er ten
Bellerin' boys and two er three
Yelpin' dawgs all on the trail
O' one little pop-eyed cottontail!

'Bout the first good fall o' snow—
So's you kin track 'em, don't you know,
Where they've run,—and one by one
Hop 'em up and chase 'em down
   And prod 'em out of a' old bresh-pile
Er a holler log they're a-hidin' roun',
      Er way en-nunder the ricked cord-wood
Er crosstie-stack by the railroad track
   'Bout a mile
Out o' sight o' the whole ding town! . . .
      Well! them's times 'at I call good!

Rabbits!—w'y, as my thoughts goes back
　　To them old boyhood days o' mine,
I kin sic him now and see "Old Jack"
A-plowin' snow in a rabbit-track
　　　And a-pitchin' over him, head and heels,
Like a blame' hat-rack,
　　As the rabbit turns fer the timber-line
　　　Down the County Ditch through the old
　　　　corn-fields. . . .

Yes, and I'll say right here to you,
　　Rabbits that boys has *earnt*, like that—
Skinned and hung fer a night er two
　　　On the old back-porch where the pump's done
　　　　froze—
Then fried 'bout right, where your brekfust's at,
With hot brown gravy and shortenin' bread,—
Rabbits, like *them*—er I ort to 'a' said,
　　I s'pose,
　　　Rabbits like *those*
Ain't so p'ticalar pore, I guess,
Fer *eatin'* purposes!

SYMPTOMS

I'M not a-workin' now!—
   I'm jes' a-layin' round
     A-lettin' *other* people plow.—
I'm cumberin' the ground! . . .
I jes' don't *keer!*—I've done my sheer
   O' sweatin'!—Anyhow,
In this dad-blasted weather here,
   I'm not a-workin' *now!*

The corn and wheat and all
   Is doin' well enough!—
They' got clean on from now tel Fall
   To show what kind o' stuff
'At's in their *own* dad-burn backbone;
   So, while the Scriptur's 'low
Man ort to reap as he have sown—
   I'm not a-workin' now!

The grass en-nunder these-
  Here ellums 'long "Old Blue,"
And shadders o' the sugar-trees,
  Beats farmin' quite a few!
As feller says,—I ruther guess
  I'll make my comp'ny bow
And *snooze* a few hours—more er less.—
  I'm not a-workin' now!

HIS PA'S ROMANCE

ALL 'at I ever want to be
Is ist to be a man like Pa
When he wuz young an' married Ma!
Uncle he told us yisterdy
Ist all about it then—'cause they,
My Pa an' Ma, wuz bofe away
To 'tend P'tracted Meetin', where
My Pa an' Ma is allus there
When all the big "Revivals" is,
An' "Love-Feasts," too, an' "Class," an' "Prayer,"
An' when's "Comoonian Servicis."
An', yes, an' Uncle said to not
To never tell *them* nor let on
Like we knowed now ist how they got
First married.   So—while they wuz gone—
Uncle he told us ever'thing—
'Bout how my Paw wuz ist a pore
Farm-boy.—He says, I tell you *what*,

Your Pa *wuz* pore!   But neighbers they
All liked him—all but one old man
An' his old wife that folks all say
Nobody liked, ner never can!

Yes, sir! an' Uncle purt' nigh swore
About the mean old man an' way
He treat' my Pa!—'cause he's a pore
Farm-hand—but prouder 'an a king—
An' ist work' on, he did, an' wore
His old patched clo'es, ist anyway,
So he saved up his wages—then
He ist worked on an' saved some more,
An' ist worked on, ist night an' day—
Till, sir, he save' up nine or ten
Er hunnerd dollars!   But he keep
All still about it, Uncle say—
But he ist thinks—an' thinks a heap!
Though what he wuz a-thinkin', Pa
He never tell' a soul but Ma—
(Then, course, you know, he wuzn't Pa,
An', course, you know, she wuzn't Ma—
They wuz ist sweethearts, course you know);
'Cause Ma wuz ist a girl, about
Sixteen; an' when my Pa he go
A-courtin' her, her Pa an' Ma—
The very first they find it out—

Wuz maddest folks you ever saw!
'Cause it wuz her old Ma an' Pa
'At hate my Pa, an' toss their head,
An' ist raise Ned!   An' her Pa said
He'd ruther see his daughter dead!
An' said she's ist a child!—an' so
Wuz Pa!—An' ef he wuz man-grown
An' only man on earth below,
His daughter shouldn't marry him
Ef he's a king an' on his throne!
Pa's chances then looked mighty slim
Fer certain, Uncle said.   But he—
He never told a soul but her
What he wuz keepin' quiet fer.
Her folks ist lived a mile from where
He lived at—an' they drove past there
To git to town.   An' ever' one
An' all the neighbors they liked her
An' showed it!   But her folks—no, sir!—
Nobody liked her parunts none!
An' so when they shet down, you know,
On Pa—an' old man tell' him so—
Pa ist went back to work, an' she
Ist waited.   An', sir! purty soon
Her folks they thought he's turned his eye
Some other way—'cause by-an'-by

They heard he'd *rented* the old place
He worked on. An' one afternoon
A neighber, that had bu'st' a trace,
He tell' the old man they wuz signs
Around the old place that the young
Man wuz a-fixin' up the old
Log cabin some, an' he had brung
New furnichur from town; an' told
How th' old house 'uz whitewashed clean
An' sweet—wiv mornin'-glory vines
An' hollyhawks all 'round the door
An' winders—an' a bran'-new floor
In th' old porch—an' wite-new green-
An'-red pump in the old sweep-well!
An', Uncle said, when he hear tell
O' all them things, the old man he
Ist grin' an' says, he "reckon' now
Some gal, er widder anyhow,
That silly boy he's coaxed at last
To marry him!" he says, says-ee,
"An' ef he has, 'so mote it be'!"
Then went back to the house to tell
His *wife* the news, as he went past
The smokehouse, an' then went on in
The kitchen, where his daughter she
Wuz washin', to tell *her*, an' grin
An' try to worry her a spell!

The mean old thing! But Uncle said
She ain't cry much—ist pull her old
Sunbonnet forrerds on her head—
So's old man he can't see her face
At all!   An' when he s'pose he scold'
An' jaw enough, he ist clear' out
An' think he's boss of all the place!

Then Uncle say, the first you know
They's go' to be a Circus-show
In town! an' old man think he'll take
His wife an' go. An' when she say
To take their daughter, too, *she* shake
Her head like she don't *want* to go;
An' when he sees she wants to stay,
The old man takes her, anyway!
An' so she went! But Uncle he
Said she looked mighty sweet that day,
Though she wuz pale as she could be,
A-speshully a-drivin' by
Wite where her beau lived at, you know;
But out the corner of his eye
The old man watch' her; but she throw
Her pairsol 'round so she can't see
The house at all! An' then she hear
Her Pa an' Ma a-talkin' low
And kind o' laughin'-like; but she

Ist set there in the seat behind,
P'tendin' like she didn't mind.
An', Uncle say, when they got past
The young man's place, an' 'pearantly
He wuzn't home, but off an' gone
To town, the old man turned at last
An' talked back to his daughter there,
All pleasant-like, from then clean on
Till they got into town, an' where
The Circus wuz, an' on inside
O' that, an' through the crowd, on to
The very top seat in the tent
Wite next the band—a-bangin' through
A tune 'at bu'st his yeers in two!
An' there the old man scrouged an' tried
To make his wife set down, an' she
A-yellin'! But ist what she meant
He couldn't hear, ner couldn't see
Till she turned 'round an' pinted. Then
He turned an' looked—an' looked again! . . .
He ist saw neighbers ever'where—
But, sir, *his daughter* wuzn't there!
An', Uncle says, he even saw
Her beau, you know, he hated so;
An' he wuz with some other girl.
An' then he heard the Clown "Haw-haw!"

An' saw the horses wheel an' whin'
Around the ring, an' heard the zipp
O' the Ringmaster's long slim whip—
But that whole Circus, Uncle said,
Wuz all inside the old man's head!

An' Uncle said, he didn't find
His daughter all that afternoon—
An' her Ma says she'll lose her mind
Ef they don't find her purty soon!
But, though they looked all day, an' stayed
There fer the night p'formance—not
No use at all!—they never laid
Their eyes on her.   An' then they got
Their team out, an' the old man shook
His fist at all the town, an' then
Shook it up at the moon ag'in,
An' said his time 'ud come, some day!
An' jerked the lines an' driv away.

Uncle, he said, he 'spect, that night,
The old man's madder yet when they
Drive past the young man's place, an' hear
A fiddle there, an' see a light
Inside, an' shadders light an' gay

A-dancin' 'crost the winder-blinds.
An' some young chaps outside yelled, "Say!
What 'pears to be the hurry—hey?"
But the old man ist whipped the lines
An' streaked past like a runaway!
An' now you'll be su'prised, I bet!—
I hardly ain't quit laughin' yet
When Uncle say, that jamboree
An' dance an' all—w'y, that's a sign
That any old man ort to see,
As plain as 8 and 1 makes 9,
That they's *a weddin'* wite inside
That very house he's whippin' so
To git apast—an', sir! the bride
There's his own daughter!   Yes, an' oh!
She's my Ma now—an' young man she
Got married, he's my Pa!   *Whoop-ee!*
But Uncle say to not laugh all
The laughin' yet, but please save some
To kind o' spice up what's to come!

Then Uncle say, about next day
The neighbors they begin to call
An' wish 'em well, an' say how glad
An' proud an' tickled ever' way
Their friends all is—an' how they had

The lovin' prayers of ever' one
That had homes of their own! But none
Said nothin' 'bout the home that she
Had run away from! So she sighed
Sometimes—an' wunst she purt' nigh cried.

Well, Uncle say, her old Pa, he
Ist like to died, he wuz so mad!
An' her Ma, too! But by-an'-by
They cool down some.
                 An' 'bout a week,
She want to see her Ma so bad,
She think she'll haf to go! An' so
She coax him; an' he kiss her cheek
An' say, Lord bless her, *course* they'll go!
An', Uncle say, when they're bofe come
A-knockin' there at her old home—
W'y, first he know, the door it flew
Open, all quick, an' she's jerked in,
An', quicker still, the door's banged to
An' locked: an' crosst the winder-sill
The old man pokes a shotgun through
An' says to git! "You stold my child,"
He says; "an', now she's back, w'y, you
Clear out, this minute, er I'll kill
You! Yes, an' I 'ull kill her, too,
Ef you don't go!" An' then, all wild,

His young wife begs him please to go!
An' so he turn' an' walk'—all slow
An' pale as death, but awful still
An' ca'm—back to the gate, an' on
Into the road, where he had gone
So many times alone, you know!
An', Uncle say, a whipperwill
Holler so lonesome, as he go
On back to'rds home, he say he 'spec'
He ist 'ud like to wring its neck!
An' I ain't think he's goin' back
All by hisse'f—but Uncle say
That's what he does, an' it's a fac'!

An' 'pears-like he's gone back to *stay*—
'Cause there he stick', ist thataway,
An' don't go nowheres any more,
Ner don't nobody ever see
Him set his foot outside the door—
Till 'bout five days, a boy loped down
The road, a-comin' past from town,
An' he called to him from the gate,
An' sent the old man word: He's thought
Things over now; an', while he hate
To lose his wife, he think she ought
To mind her Pa an' Ma an' do
Whatever *they* advise her to.

An' sends words, too, to come an' git
Her new things an' the furnichur
That he had special' bought fer her—
'Cause, now that they wuz goin' to quit,
She's free to ist have all of it;—
So, fer his love fer her, he say
To come an' git it, wite away.
An' spang! that very afternoon,
Here come her Ma—ist 'bout as soon
As old man could hitch up an 'tell
Her "hurry back!" An' 'bout as quick
As she's drove there to where my Pa—
I mean to where her son-in-law—
Lives at, he meets her at the door
All smilin', though he's awful pale
An' trimbly—like he's ist been sick;
He take her in the house—An', 'fore
She knows it, they's a cellar-door
Shet on her, an' she hears the click
Of a' old rusty padlock! Then,
Uncle, he say, she kind o' stands
An' thinks—an' thinks—an' thinks ag'in—
An' mayby thinks of her own child
Locked up—like her! An' Uncle smiled,
An' I ist laughed an' clapped my hands!

An' there she stayed! An' she can cry
Ist all she want! an' yell an' kick
To ist her heart's content! an' try
To pry out wiv a quiltin'-stick!
But Uncle say he guess at last
She 'bout give up, an' holler' through
The door-crack fer to please to be
So kind an' good as send an' tell
The old man, like she want him to,
To come, 'fore night, an' set her free,
Er—they wuz rats down there! An' yell
She did, till, Uncle say, it soured
The morning's milk in the back yard!
But all the answer reached her, where
She's skeered so in the dark down there,
Wuz ist a mutterin' that she heard—
"I've sent him word!—I've sent him word!"
An' shore enough, as Uncle say,
He *has* "sent word!"

        Well, it's plum night
An' all the house is shet up tight—
Only one winder 'bout half-way
Raised up, you know; an' ain't no light
Inside the whole house, Uncle say.

Then, first you know, there where the team
Stands hitched yet, there the old man stands—
A' old tin lantern in his hands
An' monkey-wrench; an' he don't seem
To make things out, a-standin' there.
He comes on to the gate an' feels
An' fumbles fer the latch—then hears
A voice that chills him to the heels—
"You halt! an' stand right where you air!"
Then, sir! my—my—his son-in-law,
There at the winder wiv his gun,
He tell the old man what he's done:
"You hold *my* wife a prisoner—
An' *your* wife, drat ye! I've got *her!*
An' now, sir," Uncle say he say,
"You ist turn round an' climb wite in
That wagon, an' drive home ag'in
An' bring my wife back wite away,
An' we'll trade then—an' not before
Will I unlock my cellar-door—
Not fer your wife's sake ner your own,
But *my* wife's sake—an' hers alone!"
An', Uncle say, it don't sound like
It's so, but yet it is!—He say,
From wite then, somepin' seem' to strike
The old man's funny-bone some way;

An', minute more, that team o' his
Went tearin' down the road *k'whiz!*
An' in the same two-forty style
Come whizzin' back! An' oh, that-air
Sweet girl a-cryin' all the while,
Thinkin' about her Ma there, shet
In her own daughter's cellar, where
Ist week or so *she's* kep' house there,
She hadn't time to clean it yet!
So when her Pa an' her they git
There—an' the young man grab' an' kiss
An' hug her, till she make him quit
An' ask him where her mother is.
An' then he smile' an' try to not;
Then slow-like find th' old padlock key,
An' blow a' oat-hull out of it,
An' then stoop down there where he's got
Her Ma locked up so keerfully—
An' where, wite there, he say he thought
It *ort* to been *the old man*—though
Uncle, he say, he reckon not—
When out she bounced, all tickled so
To taste fresh air ag'in an' find
Her folks wunst more, an' grab' her child
An' cry an' laugh, an' even go

An' hug the old man; an' he wind
Her in his arms, an' laugh, an' pat
Her back, an' say he's riconciled,
In such a happy scene as that,
To swap his daughter for her Ma,
An' have so smart a son-in-law
As *they* had! "Yes, an' he's my Pa!"
I laugh' an' yell', "Hooray-hooraw!"

THE RAMBO-TREE

WHEN Autumn shakes the rambo-tree—
        It's a long, sweet way across the or-
            chard!—
The bird sings low as the bumble bee—
    It's a long, sweet way across the orchard!—
The poor shote-pig he says, says he:
"When Autumn shakes the rambo-tree
There's enough for you and enough for me."—
    It's a long, sweet way across the orchard.

For just two truant lads like we,
When Autumn shakes the rambo-tree
There's enough for you and enough for me—
    It's a long, sweet way across the orchard.

When Autumn shakes the rambo-tree—
    It's a long, sweet way across the orchard!—
The mole digs out to peep and see—
    It's a long, sweet way across the orchard!—

The dusk sags down, and the moon swings free,
There's a far, lorn call, "Pig-*gee!* Pig-*gee!*"
And two boys—glad enough for three.—
　　It's a long, sweet way across the orchard.

For just two truant lads like we,
When Autumn shakes the rambo-tree
There's enough for you and enough for me—
　　It's a long, sweet way across the orchard.

THOUGHTS FER THE DISCURAGED FARMER

THE summer winds is sniffin' round the bloomin'
    locus' trees;
    And the clover in the pastur is a big day fer the
    bees,
And they been a-swiggin' honey, above board and on the
    sly,
Tel they stutter in theyr buzzin' and stagger as they fly.
The flicker on the fence-rail 'pears to jest spit on his
    wings
And roll up his feathers, by the sassy way he sings;
And the hoss-fly is a-whettin'-up his forelegs fer biz,
And the off-mare is a-switchin' all of her tale they is.

You can hear the blackbirds jawin' as they foller up the
    plow—
Oh, theyr bound to git theyr brekfast, and theyr not
    a-carin' how;
So they quarrel in the furries, and they quarrel on the
    wing—
But theyr peaceabler in pot-pies than any other thing:

319

And it's when I git my shotgun drawed up in stiddy rest,
She's as full of tribbelation as a yeller-jacket's nest;
And a few shots before dinner, when the sun's a-shinin'
    right,
Seems to kindo'-sorto' sharpen up a feller's appetite!

They's been a heap o' rain, but the sun's out to-day,
And the clouds of the wet spell is all cleared away,
And the woods is all the greener, and the grass is greener
    still;
It may rain again to-morry, but I don't think it will.
Some says the crops is ruined, and the corn's drownded
    out,
And propha-sy the wheat will be a failure, without
    doubt;
But the kind Providence that has never failed us yet,
Will be on hands onc't more at the 'leventh hour, I bet!

Does the medder-lark complane, as he swims high and
    dry
Through the waves of the wind and the blue of the sky?
Does the quail set up and whissel in a disappinted way,
Er hang his head in silunce, and sorrow all the day?

Is the chipmuck's health a-failin'?—Does he walk, er
    does he run?
Don't the buzzards ooze around up thare jest like they've
    allus done?
Is they anything the matter with the rooster's lungs er
    voice?
Ort a mortul be complainin' when dumb animals rejoice?

Then let us, one and all, be contentud with our lot;
The June is here this mornin', and the sun is shining hot.
Oh! let us fill our harts up with the glory of the day,
And banish ev'ry doubt and care and sorrow fur away!
Whatever be our station, with Providence fer guide,
Sich fine circumstances ort to make us satisfied;
Fer the world is full of roses, and the roses full of dew,
And the dew is full of heavenly love that drips fer me
    and you.

A SUMMER'S DAY

THE SUMMER'S put the idy in
 My head that I'm a boy ag'in;
 And all around's so bright and gay
I want to put my team away,
And jest git out whare I can lay
And soak my hide full of the day!
But work is work, and must be done—
Yit, as I work, I have my fun,
Jest fancyin' these furries here
Is childhood's paths onc't more so dear:—
And so I walk through medder-lands,
 And country lanes, and swampy trails
Whare long bullrushes bresh my hands;
 And, tilted on the ridered rails
Of deadnin' fences, "Old Bob White"
Whissels his name in high delight,
And whirrs away. I wunder still,
Whichever way a boy's feet will—

Whare trees has fell, with tangled tops
    Whare dead leaves shakes, I stop fer breth,
Heerin' the acorn as it drops—
    H'istin' my chin up still as deth,
And watchin' clos't, with upturned eyes,
The tree where Mr. Squirrel tries
To hide hisse'f above the limb,
But lets his own tale tell on him.
I wunder on in deeper glooms—
    Git hungry, hearin' female cries
From old farm-houses, whare perfumes
    Of harvest dinners seems to rise
And ta'nt a feller, hart and brane,
With memories he can't explane.

I wunder through the underbresh,
    Whare pig-tracks, pintin' to'rds the crick,
Is picked and printed in the fresh
    Black bottom-lands, like wimmern pick
Theyr pie-crusts with a fork, some way,
When bakin' fer camp-meetin' day.
I wunder on and on and on,
Tel my gray hair and beard is gone,
And ev'ry wrinkle on my brow
Is rubbed clean out and shaddered now
With curls as brown and fare and fine
As tenderls of the wild grape-vine

That ust to climb the highest tree
To keep the ripest ones fer me.
I wunder still, and here I am
Wadin' the ford below the dam—
The worter chucklin' round my knee
    At hornet-welt and bramble-scratch,
And me a-slippin' 'crost to see
        Ef Tyner's plums is ripe, and size
    The old man's wortermelon-patch,
        With juicy mouth and drouthy eyes.
Then, after sich a day of mirth
And happiness as worlds is wurth—
    So tired that Heaven seems nigh about,—
The sweetest tiredness on earth
    Is to git home and flatten out—
So tired you can't lay flat enugh,
And sorto' wish that you could spred
Out like molasses on the bed,
And jest drip off the aidges in
The dreams that never comes ag'in.

A TALE OF THE AIRLY DAYS

OH! TELL me a tale of the airly days—
 Of the times as they used to be;
  "Piller of Fi-er" and "Shakespeare's Plays"
 Is a' most too deep fer me!
I want plane facts, and I want plane words,
 Of the good old-fashioned ways,
When speech run free as the songs of birds
 'Way back in the airly days.

Tell me a tale of the timber-lands—
 Of the old-time pioneers;
Somepin' a pore man understands
 With his feelin's 's well as ears.
Tell of the old log house,—about
 The loft, and the puncheon flore—
The old fi-er-place, with the crane swung out,
 And the latch-string thrugh the door.

Tell of the things jest as they was—
  They don't need no excuse!—
Don't tetch 'em up like the poets does,
  Tel theyr all too fine fer use!—
Say they was 'leven in the fambily—
  Two beds, and the chist, below,
And the trundle-beds that each helt three,
  And the clock and the old bureau.

Then blow the horn at the old back-door
  Tel the echoes all halloo,
And the childern gethers home onc't more,
  Jest as they ust to do:
Blow fer Pap tel he hears and comes,
  With Tomps and Elias, too,
A-marchin' home, with the fife and drums
  And the old Red White and Blue!

Blow and blow tel the sound draps low
  As the moan of the whipperwill,
And wake up Mother, and Ruth and Jo,
  All sleepin' at Bethel Hill:
Blow and call tel the faces all
  Shine out in the back-log's blaze,
And the shadders dance on the old hewed wall
  As they did in the airly days.

UP AND DOWN OLD BRANDYWINE

U P AND DOWN old Brandywine,
  In the days 'at's past and gone—
  With a dad-burn hook-and-line
And a saplin'-pole—i swawn!
      I've had more fun, to the square
      Inch, than ever *any*where!
      Heaven to come can't discount *mine*,
      Up and down old Brandywine!

Hain't no sense in *wishin'* yit
    Wisht to goodness I *could* jes'
"Gee" the blame' world round and git
    Back to that old happiness!—
        Kind o' drive back in the shade
        "The old Covered Bridge" there laid
        'Crosst the crick, and sort o' soak
        My soul over, hub and spoke!

Honest, now!—it hain't no *dream*
　　'At I'm wantin',—but *the fac's*
As they wuz; the same old stream,
　　And the same old times, i jacks!—
　　　　Gimme back my bare feet—and
　　　　Stonebruise too!—And scratched and
　　　　　　tanned!—
　　　　And let hottest dog-days shine
　　　　Up and down old Brandywine!

In and on betwixt the trees
　　'Long the banks, pour down yer noon,
Kind o' curdled with the breeze
　　And the yallerhammer's tune;
　　　　And the smokin', chokin' dust
　　　　O' the turnpike at its wusst—
　　　　Saturd'ys, say, when it seems
　　　　Road's jes' jammed with country teams!—

Whilse the old town, fur away
　　'Crosst the hazy pastur'-land,
Dozed-like in the heat o' day
　　Peaceful' as a hired hand.
　　　　Jolt the gravel th'ough the floor
　　　　O' the old bridge!—grind and roar
　　　　With yer blame' percession-line—
　　　　Up and down old Brandywine!

Souse me and my new straw-hat
    Off the foot-log!—what *I* care?—
Fist shoved in the crown o' that—
    Like the old Clown ust to wear.—
        Wouldn't swop it fer a' old
        Gin-u-wine raal crown o' gold!—
        Keep yer *King* ef you'll gimme
        Jes' the boy I ust to be!

Spill my fishin'-worms! er steal
    My best "goggle-eye!"—but you
Can't lay hands on joys I feel
    Nibblin' like they ust to do!
        So, in memory, to-day
        Same old ripple lips away
        At my cork and saggin' line,
        Up and down old Brandywine!

There the logs is, round the hill,
    Where "Old Irvin" ust to lift
Out sunfish from daylight till
    Dewfall—'fore he'd leave "The Drift"
        And give *us* a chance—and then
        Kind o' fish back home again,
        Ketchin' 'em jes' left and right
        Where *we* hadn't got "a bite"!

Er, 'way windin' out and in,—
　　Old path th'ough the iurnweeds
And dog-fennel to yer chin—
　　Then come suddent, th'ough the reeds
　　　　And cattails, smack into where
　　　　Them-air woods-hogs ust to scare
　　　　Us clean 'crosst the County-line,
　　　　Up and down old Brandywine!

But the dim roar o' the dam
　　It 'ud coax us furder still
To'rds the old race, slow and ca'm,
　　Slidin' on to Huston's mill—
　　　　Where, I 'spect, "the Freeport crowd"
　　　　Never *warmed* to us er 'lowed
　　　　We wuz quite so overly
　　　　Welcome as we aimed to be.

Still it 'peared-like ever'thing—
　　Fur away from home as *there*—
Had more *relish*-like, i jing!—
　　Fish in stream, er bird in air!
　　　　O them rich old bottom-lands,
　　　　Past where Cowden's Schoolhouse stands!
　　　　Wortermelons—*master-mine!*
　　　　Up and down old Brandywine!

And sich pop-paws!—Lumps o' raw
 Gold and green,—jes' oozy th'ough
With ripe yaller—like you've saw
 Custard-pie with no crust to:
  And jes' *gorges* o' wild plums,
  Till a feller'd suck his thumbs
  Clean up to his elbows! *My!*—
  Me some more er lem me die!

Up and down old Brandywine!
 Stripe me with pokeberry-juice!—
Flick me with a pizen-vine
 And yell "*Yip!*" and lem me loose!
  —Old now as I then wuz young,
  'F I could sing as I *have* sung,
  Song 'ud surely ring *dee-vine*
  Up and down old Brandywine!

UNCLE DAN'L IN TOWN OVER SUNDAY

I CAIN'T git used to city ways—
  Ner ever could, I' bet my hat!
  Jevver know jes' whur I was raised?—
Raised on a farm! D' ever tell you that?
Was undoubtatly, I declare!
And now, on Sunday—fun to spare
Around a farm! Why jes' to set
Up on the top three-cornered rail
Of Pap's old place, nigh La Fayette,
I'd swap my soul off, hide and tail!
You fellers in the city here,
You don't know nothin'!—S'pose to-day,
This clatterin' Sunday, you waked up
Without no jinglin'-janglin' bells,
Ner rattlin' of the milkman's cup,
Ner any swarm of screechin' birds
Like these here English swallers—S'pose
Ut you could miss all noise like those,
And git shet o' thinkin' of 'em afterwerds,

And then, in the country, wake and hear
Nothin' but silence—wake and see
Nothin' but green woods fur and near?—
What sort o' Sunday would that be? . . .
Wisht I hed you home with me!
Now think! The laziest of all days—
To git up any time—er sleep—
Er jes' lay round and watch the haze
A-dancin' 'crost the wheat, and keep
My pipe a-goern laisurely,
And puff and whiff as pleases me—
And ef I leave a trail of smoke
Clean through the house, no one to say,
"Wah! throw that nasty thing away;
Hev some regyard fer decency!"
To walk round barefoot, if you choose;
Er saw the fiddle—er dig some bait
And go a-fishin'—er pitch hoss shoes
Out in the shade somewhurs, and wait
For dinner-time, with an appetite
Ut folks in town cain't equal quite!
To laze around the barn and poke
Fer hens' nests—er git up a match
Betwixt the boys, and watch 'em scratch

And rassle round, and sweat and swear
And quarrel to their hearts' content;
And me a-jes' a-settin' there
A-hatchin' out more devilment!
What sort o' Sunday would that be? . . .
Wisht I hed you home with me!

WHEN THE GREEN GITS BACK IN THE TREES

IN SPRING, when the green gits back in the trees,
   And the sun comes out and *stays*,
    And yer boots pulls on with a good tight squeeze,
  And you think of yer barefoot days;
When you *ort* to work and you want to *not*,
  And you and yer wife agrees
It's time to spade up the garden-lot,
  When the green gits back in the trees—
    Well! work is the least o' *my* idees
    When the green, you know, gits back in the trees!

When the green gits back in the trees, and bees
  Is a-buzzin' aroun' ag'in,
In that kind of a lazy go-as-you-please
  Old gait they bum roun' in;
When the groun's all bald where the hay-rick stood,
  And the crick's riz, and the breeze
Coaxes the bloom in the old dogwood,
  And the green gits back in the trees,—

I like, as I say, in sich scenes as these,
The time when the green gits back in the trees!

When the whole tail-feathers o' Winter-time
Is all pulled out and gone!
And the sap it thaws and begins to climb,
And the swet it starts out on
A feller's forred, a-gittin' down
At the old spring on his knees—
I kindo' like jest a-loaferin' roun'
When the green gits back in the trees—
Jest a-potterin' roun' as I—durn—please—
When the green, you know, gits back in the trees!

DOC SIFERS

OF ALL the doctors I could cite you to in this-
  'ere town
  Doc Sifers is my favorite, jes' take him up and
  down!
Count in the Bethel Neighberhood, and Rollins, and Big
  Bear,
And Sifers' standin's jes' as good as ary doctor's there!

There's old Doc Wick, and Glenn, and Hall, and
  Wurgler, and McVeigh,
But I'll buck Sifers 'g'inst 'em all and down 'em any
  day!
Most old Wick ever knowed, I s'pose, was *whisky!*
  Wurgler—well,
He et morphine—ef actions shows, and facts' reliable!

But Sifers—though he ain't no sot, he's got his faults;
  and yit
When you *git* Sifers onc't, you've got *a doctor*, don't
  fergit!

He ain't much at his office, er his house, er anywhere
You'd natchurly think certain fer to ketch the feller
    there.—

But don't blame Doc: he's got all sorts o' cur'ous no-
    tions—as
The feller says, his odd-come-shorts, like smart men
    mostly has.
He'll more'n like be potter'n' 'round the Blacksmith
    Shop; er in
Some back lot, spadin' up the ground, er gradin' it ag'in.

Er at the work bench, planin' things; er buildin' little
    traps
To ketch birds; galvenizin' rings; er graftin' plums, per-
    haps.
Make anything! good as the best!—a gun-stock—er a
    flute;
He whittled out a set o' chesstmen onc't o' laurel root,

Durin' the Army—got his trade o' surgeon there—I
    own
To-day a finger-ring Doc made out of a Sesesh bone!
An' glued a fiddle onc't fer me—jes' all so busted you
'D 'a' throwed the thing away, but he fixed her as good
    as new!

And take Doc, now, in *ager*, say, er *biles*, er *rheumatiz*,
And all afflictions thataway, and he's the best they is!
Er janders—milksick—I don't keer—k-yore anything
    he tries—
A abscess; getherin' in yer yeer; er granilated eyes!

There was the Widder Daubenspeck they all give up fer
    dead;
A blame cowbuncle on her neck, and clean out of her
    head!
First had this doctor, what's-his-name, from "Puddles-
    burg," and then
This little red-head, "Burnin' Shame" they call him—
    Dr. Glenn.

And they "consulted" on the case, and claimed she'd haf
    to die, —
I jes' was joggin' by the place, and heerd her dorter cry,
And stops and calls her to the fence; and I-says-I, "Let
    me
Send Sifers—bet you fifteen cents he'll k-yore her!"
    "Well," says she,

"Light out!" she says: And, lipp-tee-cut I loped in town,
    and rid
'Bout two hours more to find him, but I kussed him when
    I did!

He was down at the Gunsmith Shop a-stuffin' birds!
Says he,
"My sulky's broke." Says I, "You hop right on and ride
with me!"

I got him there.—"Well, Aunty, ten days k-yores you,"
Sifers said,
"But what's yer idy livin' when yer jes' as good as
dead?"
And there's Dave Banks—jes' back from war without a
scratch—one day
Got ketched up in a sickle-bar, a reaper runaway.—

His shoulders, arms, and hands and legs jes' sawed in
strips!   And Jake
Dunn starts fer Sifers—feller begs to shoot him fer God-
sake.
Doc, 'course, was gone, but he had penned the notice,
"At Big Bear—
Be back to-morry; Gone to 'tend the Bee Convention
there."

But Jake, he tracked him—rid and rode the whole endurin' night!
And 'bout the time the roosters crowed they both hove
into sight.

Doc had to ampitate, but 'greed to save Dave's arms, and
    swore
He could 'a' saved his legs ef he'd b'en there the day
    before.

Like when his wife's own mother died 'fore Sifers could
    be found,
And all the neighbers fer and wide a' all jes' chasin'
    round;
Tel finally—I had to laugh—it's jes' like Doc, you
    know,—
Was learnin' fer to telegraph, down at the old deepo.

But all they're faultin' Sifers fer, there's none of 'em
    kin say
He's biggoty, er keerless, er not posted anyway;
He ain't built on the common plan of doctors now-a-
    days,
He's jes' a great, big, brainy man—that's where the
    trouble lays!

DOWN AROUND THE RIVER

NOON-TIME and June-time, down around the
river!
Have to furse with Lizey Ann—but lawzy! I
fergive her!
Drives me off the place, and says 'at all 'at she's a-
wishin',
Land o' gracious! time'll come I'll git enough o' fishin'!
Little Dave, a-choppin' wood, never 'pears to notice;
Don't know where she's hid his hat, er keerin' where
his coat is,—
Specalatin', more'n like, he hain't a-goin' to mind me,
And guessin' where, say twelve o'clock, a feller'd likely
find me.

Noon-time and June-time, down around the river!
Clean out o' sight o' home, and skulkin' under kivver
Of the sycamores, jack-oaks, and swamp-ash and el-
lum—
Idies all so jumbled up you kin hardly tell 'em!—

Tired, you know, but *lovin'* it, and smilin' jes' to think
    'at
Any sweeter tiredness you'd fairly want to *drink* it.
Tired o' fishin'—tired o' fun—line out slack and
    slacker—
All you want in all the world's a little more tobacker!

Hungry, but *a-hidin'* it, er jes' a-not a-kerrin':—
Kingfisher gittin' up and skootin' out o' hearin';
Snipes on the t'other side, where the County Ditch is,
Wadin' up and down the aidge like they'd rolled their
    britches!
Old turkle on the root kind o' sort o' drappin'
Intoo th' worter like he don't know how it happen!
Worter, shade and all so mixed, don't know which you'd
    orter
Say, th' *worter* in the shadder—*shadder* in the *worter*.

Somebody hollerin'——'way around the bend in
Upper Fork—where yer eye kin jes' ketch the endin'
Of the shiney wedge o' wake some muss-rat's a-makin'
With that pesky nose o' his! Then a sniff o' bacon,
Corn-bread and 'dock-greens—and little Dave a-shinnin'
'Crost the rocks and mussel-shells, a-limpin' and a-
    grinnin',
With yer dinner fer ye, and a blessin' from the giver.
Noon-time and June-time down around the river!

HIS ROOM

I'M home again, my dear old Room,
  I'm home again, and happy, too,
    As, peering through the brightening gloom,
I find myself alone with you:
    Though brief my stay, nor far away,
    I missed you—missed you night and day—
    As wildly yearned for you as now.—
    Old Room, how are you, anyhow?

My easy chair, with open arms,
  Awaits me just within the door;
The littered carpet's woven charms
    Have never seemed so bright before,—
    The old rosettes and mignonettes
    And ivy-leaves and violets,
    Look up as pure and fresh of hue
    As though baptized in morning-dew.

Old Room, to me your homely walls
  Fold round me like the arms of love,
And over all my being falls
    A blessing pure as from above—

Even as a nestling child caressed
And lulled upon a loving breast,
With folded eyes, too glad to weep
And yet too sad for dreams or sleep.

You've been so kind to me, old Room—
    So patient in your tender care,
My drooping heart in fullest bloom
    Has blossomed for you unaware;
        And who but you had cared to woo
        A heart so dark, and heavy too,
        As in the past you lifted mine
        From out the shadow to the shine?

For I was but a wayward boy
    When first you gladly welcomed me
And taught me work was truer joy
    Than rioting incessantly:
        And thus the din that stormed within
        The old guitar and violin
        Has fallen in a fainter tone
        And sweeter, for your sake alone.

Though in my absence I have stood
    In festal halls a favored guest,
I missed, in this old quietude,
    My worthy work and worthy rest—

By *this* I know that long ago
You loved me first, and told me so
In art's mute eloquence of speech
The voice of praise may never reach.

For lips and eyes in truth's disguise
  Confuse the faces of my friends,
Till old affection's fondest ties
  I find unraveling at the ends;
    But, as I turn to you, and learn
    To meet my griefs with less concern,
    Your love seems all I have to keep
    Me smiling lest I needs must weep.

Yet I am happy, and would fain
  Forget the world and all its woes;
So set me to my tasks again,
  Old Room, and lull me to repose:
    And as we glide adown the tide
    Of dreams, forever side by side,
    I'll hold your hands as lovers do
    Their sweethearts' and talk love to you.

CUORED O' SKEERIN'

'LISH, you rickollect that-air
  Dad-burn skittish old bay mare
  Was no livin' with!—'at skeerd
'T ever'thing she seed er heerd!—
Th'owed 'Ves' Anders, and th'owed Pap,
First he straddled her—*k-slap!*—
And Izory—well!—th'owed *her*
Hain't no tellin' jest how fur!—
Broke her collar-bone—and **might**
Jest 'a' kilt the gyrl outright!

Course I'd heerd 'em make their boast
She th'ow any feller, 'most,
Ever topped her! S' I, "I know
One man 'at she'll never th'ow!"
So I rid her into mill,
And, jest comin' round the hill,
Met a *traction-engine!*—Ort
Jest 'a' heerd that old mare snort,
And lay back her yeers, and see
Her a-tryin' to th'ow *me!*

Course I never said a word,
But thinks I, "My ladybird,
You'll git cuored, right here and now,
Of yer dy-does anyhow!"
So I stuck her—tel she'd jest
Done her very level best;
Then I slides off—strips the lines
Over her fool-head, and finds
Me a little saplin'-gad,
'Side the road:—And there we had
Our own fun!—jest wore her out!
Mounted her, and faced about,
And jest made her *nose* that-air
Little traction-engine there!

FARMER WHIPPLE.—BACHELOR

IT'S a mystery to see me—a man o' fifty-four,
   Who's lived a cross old bachelor fer thirty year'
      and more—
A-lookin' glad and smilin'!   And they's none o' you can
   say
That you can guess the reason why I feel so good to-day!

I must tell you all about it!   But I'll have to deviate
A little in beginnin' so's to set the matter straight
As to how it comes to happen that I never took a wife—
Kind o' "crawfish" from the Present to the Spring-time
      of my life!

I was brought up in the country: Of a family of five—
Three brothers and a sister—I'm the only one alive,—
Fer they all died little babies; and 'twas one o' Mother's
      ways,
You know, to want a daughter; so she took a girl to raise.

The sweetest little thing she was, with rosy cheeks, and
      fat—

We was little chunks o' shavers then about as high as
    that!
But some way we sort o' *suited*-like! and Mother she'd
    declare
She never laid her eyes on a more lovin' pair

Than *we* was!   So we growed up side by side fer thirteen
    year',
And every hour of it she growed to me more dear!—
W'y, even Father's dyin', as he did, I do believe
Warn't more affectin' to me than it was to see her grieve!

I was then a lad o' twenty; and I felt a flash o' pride
In thinkin' all depended on *me* now to pervide
Fer Mother and fer Mary; and I went about the place
With sleeves rolled up—and workin', with a mighty
    smilin' face.—

Fer *sompin' else* was workin'! but not a word I said
Of a certain sort o' notion that was runnin' through my
    head,—
"Some day I'd maybe marry, and a *brother's* love was one
Thing—a *lover's* was another!" was the way the notion
    run!

I remember onc't in harvest, when the "cradle-in" was
    done—
(When the harvest of my summers mounted up to
    twenty-one),

I was ridin' home with Mary at the closin' o' the day—
A-chawin' straws and thinkin', in a lover's lazy way!

And Mary's cheeks was burnin' like the sunset down the
      lane:
I noticed she was thinkin', too, and ast her to explain.
Well—when she turned and *kissed* me, *with her arms
      around me—law!*
I'd a bigger load o' Heaven than I had a load o' straw!

I don't p'tend to learnin', but I'll tell you what's a fac',
They's a mighty truthful sayin' somers in a almanac—
Er *somers*—'bout "puore happiness"—perhaps some
      folk'll laugh
At the idy—"only lastin' jest two seconds and a half."—

But it's jest as true as preachin'!—fer that was a *sister's*
      kiss,
And a sister's lovin' confidence a-tellin' to me this:—
"*She* was happy, *bein' promised to the son o' farmer
      Brown.*"—
And my feelin's struck a pardnership with sunset and
      went down!

I don't know *how* I acted, I don't know *what* I said,—
Fer my heart seemed jest a-turnin' to an ice-cold lump o'
      lead;

And the hosses kind o' glimmered before me in the road,
And the lines fell from my fingers—And that was all
    I knowed—

Fer—well, I don't know *how* long—They's a dim re-
    memberence
Of a sound o' snortin' hosses, and a stake-and-ridered
    fence
A-whizzin' past, and wheat-sheaves a-dancin' in the
    air,
And Mary screamin' "Murder!" and a-runnin' up to
    where

I was layin' by the roadside, and the wagon upside down
A-leanin' on the gate-post, with the wheels a-whirlin'
    round!
And I tried to raise and meet her, but I couldn't, with a
    vague
Sort o' notion comin' to me that I had a broken leg.

Well, the women nussed me through it; but many a
    time I'd sigh
As I'd keep a-gittin' better instid o' goin' to die,
And wonder what was left *me* worth livin' fer below,
When the girl I loved was married to another, don't you
    know!

And my thoughts was as rebellious as the folks was good
    and kind
When Brown and Mary married—Railly must 'a' been
    my *mind*
Was kind o' out o' kilter!—fer I hated Brown, you see,
Worse'n *pizen*—and the feller whittled crutches out fer
    me—

And done a thousand little ac's o' kindness and respec'—
And me a-wishin' all the time that I could break his
    neck!
My relief was like a mourner's when the funeral is done
When they moved to Illinois in the Fall o' Forty-one.

Then I went to work in airnest—I had nothin' much in
    view
But to drownd out rickollections—and it kep' me busy,
    too!
But I slowly thrived and prospered, tel Mother used to
    say
She expected yit to see me a wealthy man some day.

Then I'd think how little *money* was, compared to hap-
    piness—
And who'd be left to use it when I died I couldn't guess!
But I've still kep' speculatin' and a-gainin' year by year,
Tel I'm payin' half the taxes in the county, mighty near!

Well!—A year ago er better, a letter comes to hand
Astin' how I'd like to dicker fer some Illinois land—
"The feller that had owned it," it went ahead to state,
"Had jest deceased, insolvent, leavin' chance to specu-
    late,"—

And then it closed by sayin' that I'd "better come and
    see."—
I'd never been West, anyhow—a'most too wild fer *me*,
I'd allus had a notion; but a lawyer here in town
Said I'd find myself mistakend when I come to look
    around.

So I bids good-by to Mother, and I jumps aboard the
    train,
A-thinkin' what I'd bring her when I come back home
    again—
And ef she'd had an idy what the present was to be,
I think it's more'n likely she'd 'a' went along with me!

Cars is awful tejus ridin', fer all they go so fast!
But finally they called out my stoppin'-place at last:
And that night, at the tavern, I dreamp' I was a train
O' cars, and *skeered* at somepin', runnin' down a country
    lane!

Well, in the mornin' airly—after huntin' up the man—
The lawyer who was wantin' to swap the piece o' land—
We started fer the country; and I ast the history
Of the farm—its former owner—and so forth, etcetery!

And—well—it was inter*est*in'—I su'prised him, I sup-
    pose
By the loud and frequent manner in which I blowed my
    nose!—
But his su'prise was greater, and it made him wonder
    more,
When I kissed and hugged the widder when she met us
    at the door!—

It was Mary: . . . They's a feelin' a-hidin' down in
    here—
Of course I can't explain it, ner ever make it clear.—
It was with us in that meetin', I don't want you to fergit!
And it makes me kind o' nervous when I think about it
    yit!

I *bought* that farm, and *deeded* it, afore I left the town,
With "title clear to mansions in the skies," to Mary
    Brown!
And fu'thermore, I took her and the *childern*—fer you
    see,
They'd never seed their Grandma—and I fetched 'em
    home with me.

So *now* you've got an idy why a man o' fifty-four,
Who's lived a cross old bachelor fer thirty year' and
    more,
Is a-lookin' glad and smilin'!—And I've jest come into
    town
To git a pair o' license fer to *marry* Mary Brown.

'MONGST THE HILLS O' SOMERSET

'MONGST the Hills o' Somerset
 Wisht I was a-roamin' yet!
 My feet won't get usen to
These low lands I'm trompin' through.
Wisht I could go back there, and
Stroke the long grass with my hand,
Kind o' like my sweetheart's hair
Smoothed out underneath it there!
Wisht I could set eyes once more
On our shadders, on before,
Climbin', in the airly dawn,
Up the slopes 'at love growed on
Natchurl as the violet
'Mongst the Hills o' Somerset!

How 't 'u'd rest a man like me
Jes' fer 'bout an hour to be
Up there where the morning air
Could reach out and ketch me there!—
Snatch my breath away, and then
Rensh and give it back again

357

Fresh as dew, and smellin' of
The old pinks I ust to love,
And a-flavor'n' ever' breeze
With mixt hints o' mulberries
And May-apples, from the thick
Bottom-lands along the crick
Where the fish bit, dry er wet,
'Mongst the Hills o' Somerset!

Like a livin' pictur' things
All comes back: the bluebird swings
In the maple, tongue and bill
Trillin' glory fit to kill!
In the orchard, jay and bee
Ripens the first pears fer me,
And the "Prince's Harvest" they
Tumble to me where I lay
In the clover, provin' still
"A boy's will is the wind's will."
Clean fergot is time, and care,
And thick hearin', and gray hair—
But they's nothin' I ferget
'Mongst the Hills o' Somerset!

Middle-aged—to be edzact,
Very middle-aged, in fact,—

Yet a-thinkin' back to then,
I'm the same wild boy again!
There's the dear old home once more,
And there's Mother at the door—
Dead, I know, fer thirty year',
Yet she's singin', and I hear;
And there's Jo, and Mary Jane,
And Pap, comin' up the lane!
Dusk's a-fallin'; and the dew,
'Pears like, it's a-fallin' too—
Dreamin' we're all livin' yet
'Mongst the Hills o' Somerset!

OLD JOHN HENRY

OLD John's jes' made o' the commonest stuff—
  Old John Henry—
    He's tough, I reckon,—but none too tough—
Too tough though's better than not enough!
    Says old John Henry.
He does his best, and when his best's bad,
He don't fret none, ner he don't git sad—
He simply 'lows it's the best he had:
    Old John Henry!

His doctern's jes' o' the plainest brand—
    Old John Henry—
A smilin' face and a hearty hand
'S religen 'at all folks understand,
    Says old John Henry.
He's stove up some with the rhumatiz,
And they hain't no shine on them shoes o' his,
And his hair hain't cut—but his eye-teeth is:
    Old John Henry!

He feeds hisse'f when the stock's all fed—
    Old John Henry—
And sleeps like a babe when he goes to bed—
And dreams o' Heaven and home-made bread,
    Says old John Henry.
He hain't refined as he'd ort to be
To fit the statutes o' poetry,
Ner his clothes don't fit him—but *he* fits *me:*
    Old John Henry!

"HOME AG'IN"

I'M a-feelin' ruther sad,
    Fer a father proud and glad
    As *I* am—my only child
Home, and all so rickonciled!
Feel so strange-like, and don't know
What the mischief ails me so!
'Stid o' bad, I ort to be
Feelin' good pertickerly—
Yes, and extry thankful, too,
'Cause my nearest kith and kin,
My Elviry's schoolin' 's through,
And I' got her home ag'in—
        Home ag'in with me!

Same as ef her mother'd been
Livin', I have done my best
By the girl, and watchfulest;
Nussed her—keerful' as I could—
From a baby, day and night,—
Drawin' on the neighberhood
And the women-folks as light

362

As needsessity 'ud 'low—
'Cept in "teethin'," onc't, and fight
Through black-measles. Don't know now
How we ever saved the child!
Doc *he'd* give her up, and said,
As I stood there by the bed
Sort o' foolin' with her hair
On the hot, wet pillar there,
"Wuz no use!"—And at them-air
Very words she waked and smiled—
Yes, and *knowed* me. And that's where
I broke down, and simply jes'
Bellered like a boy—I guess!—
Women claim I did, but I
Allus helt I didn't cry
But wuz laughin',—and I *wuz*,—
Men don't cry like *women* does!
Well, right then and there I felt
'T 'uz her mother's doin's, and,
Jes' like to mys'f, I knelt
Whisperin', "I understand." . . .
So I've raised her, you might say,
Stric'ly in the narrer way
'At her mother walked therein—
Not so quite religiously,

Yit still strivin'-like to do
Ever'thing a father *could*
Do he knowed the *mother* would
Ef she'd lived—And now all's through
And I' got her home ag'in—
  Home ag'in with me!

And I' been so lonesome, too,
Here o' late, especially,—
"Old Aunt Abigail," you know,
Ain't no company;—and so
Jes' the hired hand, you see—
Jonas—like a relative
More—sence he come here to live
With us, nigh ten year' ago.
Still he don't count much, you know,
In the way o' company—
Lonesome, 'peared-like, 'most as me!
So, as *I* say, I' been so
Special lonesome-like and blue,
With Elviry, like she's been,
'Way so much, last two or three
Year'—But now she's home ag'in—
  Home ag'in with me!
Driv in fer her yisterday,
Me and Jonas—gay and spry,—
We jes' cut up, all the way!—

Yes, and sung!—tel, blame it! I
Keyed my voice up 'bout as high
As when—days 'at I wuz young—
"Buckwheat-notes" wuz all they sung.
Jonas bantered me, and 'greed
To sing one 'at town-folks sing
Down at Split Stump 'er High-Low—
Some new "ballet," said he, 'at he'd
Learnt—about "The Grape-vine Swing."
And when *he* quit, *I* begun
To chune up my voice and run
Through the what's-called "scales" and "do
Sol-me-fa's" I *ust* to know—
Then let loose old favor*ite* one,
"Hunters o' Kentucky!" *My!*
Tel I thought the boy would *die!*
And we *both* laughed—Yes, and still
Heerd more laughin', top the hill;
Fer we'd missed Elviry's train,
And she'd lit out 'crost the fields,—
Dewdrops dancin' at her heels,
And cut up old Smoots's lane
So's to meet us. And there in
Shadder o' the chinkypin,
With a danglin' dogwood-bough
Bloomin' 'bove her—See her now!—
Sunshine sort o' flickerin' down

And a kind o' laughin' all
Round her new red parasol,
Tryin' to git at *her!*—well—like
I jumped out and showed 'em how—
Yes, and jes' the place to strike
That-air mouth o' hern—as sweet
As the blossoms breshed her brow
Er sweet-williams round her feet—
White and blushy, too, as she
"Howdied" up to Jonas, and
Jieuked her head, and waved her hand.
"Hey!" says I, as she bounced in
The spring-wagon, reachin' back
To give *me* a lift, "whoop-ee!"
I-says-ee, "you're home ag'in—
　　　Home ag'in with me!"

Lord! how *wild* she wuz, and glad,
Gittin' home!—and things she had
To inquire about, and talk—
Plowin', plantin', and the stock—
News o' neighborhood; and how
Wuz the Deem-girls doin' now,
Sence that-air young chicken-hawk
They was "tamin'" soared away
With their settin'-hen, one day?—

(Said she'd got Mame's postal-card
'Bout it, very day 'at she
Started home from Bethany.)
How wuz produce—eggs, and lard?—
Er wuz stores still claimin' "hard
Times," as usual?   And, says she,
Troubled-like, "How's Deedie—say?
Sence pore child e-loped away
And got back, and goin' to 'ply
Fer school-license by and by—
And where's 'Lijy workin' at?
And how's 'Aunt' and 'Uncle Jake'?
How wuz 'Old Maje'—and the cat?
And wuz Marthy's baby fat
As his 'Humpty-Dumpty' ma?
Sweetest thing she ever saw!—
Must run 'crost and see her, too,
Soon as she turned in and got
Supper fer us—smokin'-hot—
And the 'dishes' all wuz through.—"
Sich a supper! W'y, I set
There and et, and et, and et!—
Jes' et on, tel Jonas he
Pushed his chair back, laughed, and says,
"I could walk *his* log!" and we
All laughed then, tel 'Viry she

Lit the lamp—and I give in!—
Riz and kissed her: "Heaven bless
You!" says I—"you're home ag'in—
Same old dimple in your chin,
Same white apern," I-says-ee,
"Same sweet girl, and good to see
As your *mother* ust to be,—
And I' got you home ag'in—
        Home ag'in with me!"

I turns then to go on by her
Through the door—and see her eyes
Both wuz swimmin', and she tries
To say somepin'—can't—and so
Grabs and hugs and lets me go.
Noticed Aunty'd made a fire
In the settin'-room and gone
Back where her p'serves wuz on
Bilin' in the kitchen. I
Went out on the porch and set,
Thinkin'-like. And by and by
Heerd Elviry, soft and low,
At the organ, kind o' go
A mi-anderin' up and down
With her fingers 'mongst the keys—
"Vacant Chair" and "Old Camp-Groun'." . . .

Dusk was moist-like, with a breeze
Lazin' round the locus'-trees—
Heerd the hosses champin', and
Jonas feedin', and the hogs—
Yes, and katydids and frogs—
And a tree-toad, somers. Heerd
Also whipperwills.—*My land!*—
All so mournful ever'where—
Them out here, and her in there,—
'Most like 'tendin' *services!*
Anyway, I must 'a' jes
Kind o' drapped asleep, I guess;
'Cause when Jonas must 'a' passed
Me, a-comin' in, I knowed
Nothin' of it—yit it seemed
Sort o' like I kind o' dreamed
'Bout him, too, a-slippin' in,
And a-watchin' back to see
Ef I *wuz* asleep, and then
Passin' in where 'Viry wuz;
And where I declare it does
'Pear to me I heerd him say,
Wild and glad and whisperin'—
'Peared-like heerd him say, says-ee,
"Ah! I got you home ag'in—
        Home ag'in with me!"

CASSANDER

"CASSANDER! *O* Cassander!"—her *mother's
    voice* seems cle'r
        As ever, from the old back-porch, a-hollerin'
            fer her—
Specially in airly Spring—like May, two year' ago—
Last time she hollered fer her,—and Cassander didn't
    hear!

Cassander wuz so chirpy-like and sociable and free,
And good to ever'body, and wuz even good to me
    Though *I* wuz jes' a common—well, a farm-hand,
        don't you know,
A-workin' on her father's place, as pore as pore could be!

Her bein' jes' a' only child, Cassander had her way
A good-'eal more'n other girls; and neighbers ust to say
    She looked most like her Mother, but wuz turned most
        like her Pap,—
Except *he* had no use fer *town*-folks then—ner *yit* to-
    day!

I can't claim she incouraged *me:* She'd let me drive her
in
To town sometimes, on Saturd'ys, and fetch her home
ag'in,
Tel onc't she 'scused "Old Moll" and me,—and some
blame' city-chap,
He driv her home, two-forty style, in face o' kith and
kin.

She even tried to make him stay fer supper, but I 'low
He must 'a' kind o' 'spicioned some objections.—Anyhow,
Her mother callin' at her, whilse her father stood and
shook
His fist,—the town-chap turnt his team and made his
partin' bow.

"Cassander! *You,* Cassander!"—hear her mother jes'
as plain,
And see Cassander blushin' like the peach-tree down the
lane,
Whilse I sneaked on apast her, with a sort o' hang-dog
look,
A-feelin' cheap as sorghum and as green as sugar-cane!

(You see, I'd *skooted* when she met her *town*-beau—
     when, in fact,
Ef I'd had sense I'd *stayed* fer her.—But sense wuz what
     I lacked!
   So I'd cut home ahead o' her, so's I could tell 'em what
Wuz keepin' her.   And—*you* know how a jealous fool'll
     act!)

I past her, I wuz sayin',—but she never turnt her head;
I swallered-like and cle'red my th'oat—but that wuz all
     I said;
   And whilse I hoped fer some word back, it wuzn't
     what I got.—
That girl'll not stay stiller on the day she's layin' dead!

Well, that-air silence *lasted!*—Ust to listen ever' day
I'd be at work and hear her mother callin' thataway;
   I'd *sight* Cassander, mayby, cuttin' home acrost the
     blue
And drizzly fields; but nary answer—nary word to say!

Putt in about two weeks o' that—two weeks o' rain and
     mud,
Er mostly so: I couldn't plow.   The old crick like a
     flood:

And, lonesome as a borried dog, I'd wade them old
  woods through—
The dogwood blossoms white as snow, and redbuds red
  as blood.

Last time her mother called her—sich a morning like as
    now:
The robins and the bluebirds, and the blossoms on the
    bough—
  And this wuz yit 'fore brekfust, with the sun out at
    his best,
And hosses kickin' in the barn—and dry enough to plow.

"Cassander! *O* Cassander!" ... And her only answer—
    What?—
A letter, twisted round the cookstove damper, smokin'-
    hot,
  A-statin': "I wuz married on that day of all the rest,
The day my husband fetched me home—ef you ain't all
    fergot!"

"Cassander! *O* Cassander!" seems, allus, 'long in May,
I hear her mother callin' her—a-callin', night and day—
  "Cassander! *O* Cassander!" allus callin', as I say,
"Cassander! *O* Cassander!" jes a-callin' thataway.

WE MUST GET HOME

WE MUST get home! How could we stray
like this?—
So far from home, we know not where it
is,—
Only in some fair, apple-blossomy place
Of children's faces—and the mother's face—
We dimly dream it, till the vision clears
Even in the eyes of fancy, glad with tears.

We must get home—for we have been away
So long, it seems forever and a day!
And O so very homesick we have grown,
The laughter of the world is like a moan
In our tired hearing, and its songs as vain,—
We must get home—we must get home again!

We must get home!   With heart and soul we yearn
To find the long-lost pathway, and return! . . .
The child's shout lifted from the questing band
Of old folk, faring weary, hand in hand,

But faces brightening, as if clouds at last
Were showering sunshine on us as they passed.

We must get home: It hurts so, staying here,
Where fond hearts must be wept out tear by tear,
And where to wear wet lashes means, at best,
When most our lack, the least our hope of rest—
When most our need of joy, the more our pain—
We must get home—we must get home again!

We must get home—home to the simple things—
The morning-glories twirling up the strings
And bugling color, as they blared in blue-
And-white o'er garden-gates we scampered through;
The long grape-arbor, with its under-shade
Blue as the green and purple overlaid.

We must get home: All is so quiet there:
The touch of loving hands on brow and hair—
Dim rooms, wherein the sunshine is made mild—
The lost love of the mother and the child
Restored in restful lullabies of rain,—
We must get home—we must get home again!

The rows of sweetcorn and the China beans
Beyond the lettuce-beds where, towering, leans

The giant sunflower in barbaric pride
Guarding the barn-door and the lane outside;
The honeysuckles, midst the hollyhocks,
That clamber almost to the martin-box.

We must get home, where, as we nod and drowse,
Time humors us and tiptoes through the house,
And loves us best when sleeping baby-wise,
With dreams—not tear-drops—brimming our clenched
    eyes,—
Pure dreams that know nor taint nor earthly stain—
We must get home—we must get home again!

We must get home! There only may we find
The little playmates that we left behind,—
Some racing down the road; some by the brook;
Some droning at their desks, with wistful look
Across the fields and orchards—farther still
Where laughs and weeps the old wheel at the mill.

We must get home! The willow-whistle's call
Trills crisp and liquid as the waterfall—
Mocking the trillers in the cherry-trees
And making discord of such rhymes as these,
That know nor lilt nor cadence but the birds
First warbled—then all poets afterwards.

We must get home; and, unremembering there
All gain of all ambition otherwhere,
Rest—from the feverish victory, and the crown
Of conquest whose waste glory weighs us down.—
Fame's fairest gifts we toss back with disdain—
We must get home—we must get home again!

We must get home again—we must—we must!—
(Our rainy faces pelted in the dust)
Creep back from the vain quest through endless strife
To find not anywhere in all of life
A happier happiness than blest us then. . . .
We must get home—we must get home again!

US FARMERS IN THE COUNTRY

US FARMERS in the country, as the seasons go
        and come,
    Is purty much like other folks,—we're apt to
        grumble some!
The Spring's too back'ard fer us, er too for'ard—ary
    one—
We'll jaw about it anyhow, and have our way er none!

The thaw's set in too suddent; er the frost's stayed in the
    soil
Too long to give the wheat a chance, and crops is bound
    to spoil.
The weather's eether most too mild, er too outrageous
    rough,
And altogether too much rain, er not half rain enugh!

Now what I'd like and what you'd like is plane enugh to
    see:
It's jest to have old Providence drop round on you and me
And ast us what our views is first, regardin' shine er rain,
And post 'em when to shet her off, er let her on again!

And yit I'd ruther, after all—consider'n' other chores
I' got on hands, a-tendin' both to my affares and yours—
I'd ruther miss the blame I'd git, a-rulin' things up thare,
And spend my extry time in praise and gratitude and
prayer.

A CHILD'S HOME—LONG AGO

EVEN as the gas-flames flicker to and fro,
   The Old Man's wavering fancies leap and
     glow—
As o'er the vision, like a mirage, falls
The old log cabin with its dingy walls,
And crippled chimney with its crutch-like prop
Beneath a sagging shoulder at the top:
The coonskin battened fast on either side—
The wisps of leaf-tobacco—"cut-and-dried";
The yellow strands of quartered apples, hung
In rich festoons that tangle in among
The morning-glory vines that clamber o'er
The little clapboard roof above the door:
The old well-sweep that drops a courtesy
To every thirsting soul so graciously,
The stranger, as he drains the dripping gourd,
Intuitively murmurs, "Thank the Lord!"
Again through mists of memory arise
The simple scenes of home before the eyes:—
The happy mother, humming, with her wheel,
The dear old melodies that used to steal

So drowsily upon the summer air,
The house-dog hid his bone, forgot his care,
And nestled at her feet, to dream, perchance,
Some cooling dream of winter-time romance:
The square of sunshine through the open door
That notched its edge across the puncheon floor,
And made a golden coverlet whereon
The god of slumber had a picture drawn
Of Babyhood, in all the loveliness
Of dimpled cheek and limb and linsey dress:
The bough-filled fireplace, and the mantel wide,
Its fire-scorched ankles stretched on either side,
Where, perched upon its shoulders 'neath the joist,
The old clock hiccoughed, harsh and husky-voiced,
And snarled the premonition, dire and dread,
When it should hammer Time upon the head:
Tomatoes, red and yellow, in a row,
Preserved not then for diet, but for show,—
Like rare and precious jewels in the rough
Whose worth was not appraised at half enough:
The jars of jelly, with their dusty tops;
The bunch of pennyroyal; the cordial drops;
The flask of camphor, and the vial of squills,
The box of buttons, garden-seeds, and pills;
And, ending all the mantel's bric-à-brac,
The old, time-honored "Family Almanack."

And memory, with a mother's touch of love,
Climbs with us to the dusky loft above,
Where drowsily we trail our fingers in
The mealy treasures of the harvest bin;
And, feeling with our hands the open track,
We pat the bag of barley on the back;
And, groping onward through the mellow gloom,
We catch the hidden apple's faint perfume,
And, mingling with it, fragrant hints of pear
And musky melon ripening somewhere.
Again we stretch our limbs upon the bed
Where first our simple childish prayers were said;
And while, without, the gallant cricket trills
A challenge to the solemn whippoorwills,
And, filing on the chorus with his glee,
The katydid whets all the harmony
To feather-edge of incoherent song,
We drop asleep, and peacefully along
The current of our dreams we glide away
To the dim harbor of another day.

A VOICE FROM THE FARM

IT IS my dream to have you here with me,
   Out of the heated city's dust and din—
   Here where the colts have room to gambol in,
And kine to graze, in clover to the knee.
I want to see your wan face happily
   Lit with the wholesome smiles that have not been
   In use since the old games you used to win
When we pitched horseshoes: And I want to be
   At utter loaf with you in this dim land
      Of grove and meadow, while the crickets make
         Our own talk tedious, and the bat wields
His bulky flight, as we cease converse and
      In a dusk like velvet smoothly take
         Our way toward home across the dewy fields.

HOME-FOLKS

HOME-FOLKS!—Well, that-air name, to me
  Sounds jis the same as *poetry*—
  That is, ef poetry is jis
As sweet as I've hearn tell it is!

Home-Folks—they're jis the same as *kin*—
All brung up, same as *we* have bin,
Without no overpowerin' sense
Of their oncommon consequence!

They've bin to school, but not to git
The habit fastened on 'em yit
So as to ever interfere
With *other* work 'at's waitin' here:

Home-Folks has crops to plant and plow,
Er lives in town and keeps a cow;
But whether country-jakes er town-,
They know when eggs is up er down!

La! can't you *spot* 'em—when you meet
'Em *anywheres*—in field er street?
And can't you see their faces, bright
As circus-day, heave into sight?

And can't you hear their "Howdy!" clear
As a brook's chuckle to the ear,
And allus find their laughin' eyes
As fresh and clear as morning skies?

And can't you—when they've gone away
Jis feel 'em shakin' hands, all day?
And feel, too, you've bin higher raised
By sich a meetin'?—God be praised!

Oh, Home-Folks! you're the best of all
'At ranges this terreschul ball,—
But, north er south, er east er west,
It's home is where you're at your best.—

It's home—it's home your faces shine,
In-nunder your own fig and vine—
Your fambly and your neighbers 'bout
Ye, and the latch-string hangin' out

.   .   .   .

Home-Folks—*at home*,—I know o' one
Old feller now 'at hain't got none.—
Invite him—he may hold back some—
But *you* invite him, and he'll come.

385

THE HOOSIER FOLK-CHILD

THE Hoosier Folk-Child—all unsung—
    Unlettered all of mind and tongue;
    Unmastered, unmolested—made
Most wholly frank and unafraid:
Untaught of any school—unvexed
Of law or creed—all unperplexed—
Unsermoned, ay, and undefiled,
An all imperfect-perfect child—
A type which (Heaven forgive us!) you
And I do tardy honor to,
And so profane the sanctities
Of our most sacred memories.
Who, growing thus from boy to man,
That dares not be American?
Go, Pride, with prudent underbuzz—
Go *whistle!* as the Folk-Child does.

The Hoosier Folk-Child's world is not
Much wider than the stable-lot
Between the house and highway fence
That bounds the home his father rents.

His playmates mostly are the ducks
And chickens, and the boy that "shucks
Corn by the shock," and talks of town,
And whether eggs are "up" or "down,"
And prophesies in boastful tone
Of "owning horses of his own,"
And "being his own man," and "when
He gets to be, what he'll do then."—
Takes out his jack-knife dreamily
And makes the Folk-Child two or three
Crude corn-stalk figures,—a wee span
Of horses and a little man.

The Hoosier Folk-Child's eyes are wise
And wide and round as Brownies' eyes:
The smile they wear is ever blent
With all-expectant wonderment,—
On homeliest things they bend a look
As rapt as o'er a picture-book,
And seem to ask, whate'er befall,
The happy reason of it all:—
Why grass is all so glad a green,
And leaves—and what their lispings mean;—
Why buds grow on the boughs, and why
They burst in blossom by and by—
As though the orchard in the breeze
Had shook and popped its *pop-corn trees,*

To lure and whet, as well they might,
Some seven-league giant's appetite!

The Hoosier Folk-Child's chubby face
Has scant refinement, caste or grace,—
From crown to chin, and cheek to cheek,
It bears the grimy water-streak
Of rinsings such as some long rain
Might drool across the window-pane
Wherethrough he peers, with troubled frown,
As some lorn team drives by for town.
His brow is elfed with wispish hair,
With tangles in it here and there,
As though the warlocks snarled it so
At midmirk when the moon sagged low,
And boughs did toss and skreek and shake,
And children moaned themselves awake,
With fingers clutched, and starting sight
Blind as the blackness of the night!

The Hoosier Folk-Child!—Rich is he
In all the wealth of poverty!
He owns nor title nor estate,
Nor speech but half articulate,—
He owns nor princely robe nor crown;—
Yet, draped in patched and faded brown,
He owns the bird-songs of the hills—
The laughter of the April rills;

And his are all the diamonds set
In Morning's dewy coronet,—
And his the Dusk's first minted stars
That twinkle through the pasture-bars
And litter all the skies at night
With glittering scraps of silver light;—
The rainbow's bar, from rim to rim,
In beaten gold, belongs to him.

WHAT SMITH KNEW ABOUT FARMING

THERE wasn't two purtier farms in the state
    Than the couple of which I'm about to relate;—
    Jinin' each other—belongin' to Brown,
And jest at the edge of a flourishin' town.
Brown was a man, as I understand,
That allus had handled a good 'eal o' land,
And was sharp as a tack in drivin' a trade—
For that's the way most of his money was made.
And all the grounds and the orchards about
His two pet farms was all tricked out
With poppies and posies
And sweet-smellin' rosies;
And hundreds o' kinds
Of all sorts o' vines,
To tickle the most horticultural minds;
And little dwarf trees not as thick as your wrist
With ripe apples on 'em as big as your fist:
And peaches,—Siberian crabs and pears,
And quinces—Well! *any* fruit *any* tree bears;
And the purtiest stream—jest a-swimmin' with fish,
And—*jest a'most everything heart could wish!*

The purtiest orch'rds—I wish you could see
How purty they was, fer I know it 'ud be
A regular treat!—but I'll go ahead with
My story!   A man by the name o' Smith—
(A bad name to rhyme,
But I reckon that I'm
Not goin' back on a Smith! nary time!)
'At hadn't a soul of kin nor kith,
And more money than he knowed what to do with,—
So he comes a-ridin' along one day,
And *he* says to Brown, in his offhand way—
Who was trainin' some newfangled vines round a bay-
Winder—"Howdy-do—look-a-here—say:
What'll you take fer this property here?—
I'm talkin' o' leavin' the city this year,
And I want to be
Where the air is free,
And I'll *buy* this place, if it ain't too dear!"—
Well—they grumbled and jawed aroun'—
"I don't like to part with the place," says Brown;
"Well," says Smith, a-jerkin' his head,
"That house yonder—bricks painted red—
Jest like this'n—a *purtier view*—
Who is it owns *it?*" "That's mine too,"
Says Brown, as he winked at a hole in his shoe,
"But I'll tell you right here jest what I *kin* do:—
If you'll pay the figgers I'll sell *it* to you."

Smith went over and looked at the place—
Badgered with Brown, and argied the case—
Thought that Brown's figgers was rather too tall,
But, findin' that Brown wasn't goin' to fall,
In final agreed,
So they drawed up the deed
Fer the farm and the fixtures—the live stock an' all.
And so Smith moved from the city as soon
As he possibly could—But "the man in the moon"
Knowed more'n Smith o' farmin' pursuits,
And jest to convince you, and have no disputes,
How little he knowed,
I'll tell you his "mode,"
As he called it, o' raisin' "the best that growed,"
In the way o' potatoes—
Cucumbers—tomatoes,
And squashes as lengthy as young alligators.
'Twas allus a curious thing to me
How big a fool a feller kin be
When he gits on a farm after leavin' a town!—
Expectin' to raise himself up to renown,
And reap fer himself agricultural fame,
By growin' of squashes—*without any shame*—
As useless and long as a technical name.
To make the soil pure,
And certainly sure,
He plastered the ground with patent manure.

He had cultivators, and double-hoss plows,
And patent machines fer milkin' his cows;
And patent hay-forks—patent measures and weights,
And new patent back-action hinges fer gates,
And barn locks and latches, and such little dribs
And patents to keep the rats out o' the cribs—
Reapers and mowers,
And patent grain sowers;
And drillers
And tillers
And cucumber hillers,
And harriers;—and had patent rollers and scrapers,
And took about ten agricultural papers.
So you can imagine how matters turned out:
But *Brown* didn't have not a shadder o' doubt
That Smith didn't know what he was about
When he said that "the *old* way to farm was played out."
But Smith worked ahead,
And when any one said
That the *old* way o' workin' was better instead
O' his "modern idees," he allus turned red,
And wanted to know
What made people so
Infernally anxious to hear theirselves crow?
And guessed that he'd manage to hoe his own row.
Brown he come onc't and leant over the fence,
And told Smith that he couldn't see any sense

In goin' to such a tremendous expense
Fer the sake o' such no-account expeeriments:—
"That'll never make corn!
As shore's you're born
It'll come out the leetlest end of the horn!"
Says Brown, as he pulled off a big roastin'-ear
From a stalk of his own
That had tribble outgrown
Smith's poor yaller shoots, and says he, "Looky here!
This corn was raised in the old-fashioned way,
And I rather imagine that *this* corn'll pay
Expenses fer *raisin'* it!—What do you say?"
Brown got him then to look over his crop.—
His luck that season had been tip-top!
And you may surmise
Smith opened his eyes
And let out a look o' the wildest surprise
When Brown showed him punkins as big as the lies
He was stuffin' him with—about offers he's had
Fer his farm: "I don't want to sell very bad,"
He says, but says he,
"Mr. Smith, you kin see
Fer yourself how matters is standin' with me,
I understand farmin' and I'd better stay,
You know, on my farm;—I'm a-makin' it pay—

I oughtn't to grumble!—I reckon I'll clear
Away over four thousand dollars this year."
And that was the reason, he made it appear,
Why he didn't care about sellin' his farm,
And hinted at his havin' done himself harm
In sellin' the other, and wanted to know
If Smith wouldn't sell back ag'in to him.—So
Smith took the bait, and says he, "Mr. Brown,
I wouldn't *sell* out, but we might swap aroun'—
How'll you trade your place fer mine?"
(Purty sharp way o' comin' the shine
Over Smith! Wasn't it?) Well, sir, this Brown
Played out his hand and brought Smithy down—
Traded with him an', workin' it cute,
Raked in two thousand dollars to boot
As slick as a whistle, an' that wasn't all,—
He managed to trade back ag'in the next fall,
And the next—and the next—as long as Smith stayed
He reaped with his harvests an annual trade.—
Why, I reckon that Brown must 'a' easily made—
On an *average*—nearly two thousand a year—
Together he made over seven thousand—clear.—
Till Mr. Smith found he was losin' his health
In as big a proportion, almost, as his wealth;

So at last he concluded to move back to town,
And sold back his farm to this same Mr. Brown
At very low figgers, by gittin' it down.
Further'n this I have nothin' to say
Than merely advisin' the Smiths fer to stay
In their grocery stores in flourishin' towns
And leave agriculture alone—and the Browns.

HOME AT NIGHT

WHEN chirping crickets fainter cry,
  And pale stars blossom in the sky,
  And twilight's gloom has dimmed the bloom
And blurred the butterfly:

When locust-blossoms fleck the walk,
And up the tiger-lily stalk
The glow-worm crawls and clings and falls
And glimmers down the garden-walls:

When buzzing things, with double wings
Of crisp and raspish flutterings,
Go whizzing by so very nigh
One thinks of fangs and stings:—

O then, within, is stilled the din
Of crib she rocks the baby in,
And heart and gate and latch's weight
Are lifted—and the lips of Kate.

A CANARY AT THE FARM

FOLKS has be'n to town, and Sahry
    Fetched 'er home a pet canary,—
    And of all the blame', contrary,
      Aggervatin' things alive!
I love music—that's I love it
When it's *free*—and plenty of it;—
But I kindo' git above it,
      At a dollar-eighty-five!

Reason's plain as I'm a-sayin'—
Jes' the idy, now, o' layin'
Out yer money, and a-payin'
      Fer a willer-cage and bird,
When the medder-larks is wingin'
Round you, and the woods is ringin'
With the beautifullest singin'
      That a mortal ever heard!

Sahry's sot, tho'.—So I tell her
He's a purty little feller,
With his wings o' creamy-yeller,
    And his eyes keen as a cat;
And the twitter o' the critter
'Pears to absolutely glitter!
Guess I'll haf to go and git her
    A high-priceter cage 'n that!

HOOSIER SPRING-POETRY

WHEN ever'thing's a-goin' like she's got-a-
goin' now,—
The maple-sap a-drippin', and the buds on
ever' bough
A-sort o' reachin' up'ards all a-trimblin', ever' one,
Like 'bout a million brownie-fists a-shakin' at the sun!
The childern wants their shoes off 'fore their breakfast,
and the Spring
Is here so good-and-plenty that the old hen has to sing!—
When things is goin' *thisaway*, w'y, that's the sign, you
know,
That ever'thing's a-goin' like we like to see her go!

Oh, ever'thing's a-goin' like we like to see her go!
Old Winter's up and dusted, with his dratted frost and
snow—
The ice is out the crick ag'in, the freeze is out the ground,
And you'll see faces thawin' too ef you'll jes' look
around!—

The bluebird's landin' home ag'in, and glad to git the
   chance,
'Cause here's where he belongs at, that's a settled circum-
   stance!
And him and mister robin now's a-chunin' fer the show.
Oh, ever'thing's a-goin' like we like to see her go!

The sun ain't jes' p'tendin' *now*!—The ba'm is in the
   breeze—
The trees'll soon be green as grass, and grass as green as
   trees;
The buds is all jes' *eechin'*, and the dogwood down the
   run
Is bound to bu'st out laughin' 'fore another week is done;
The bees is wakin', gap'y-like, and fumblin' fer their
   buzz,
A-thinkin', ever-wakefuler, of other days that wuz,—
When all the land wuz orchard-blooms and clover, don't
   you know. . . .
Oh, ever'thing's a-goin' like we like to see her go!

ON THE BANKS O' DEER CRICK

O N THE banks o' Deer Crick!   There's the place
      fer me!—
         Worter slidin' past ye jes' as clair as it kin be:
See yer shadder in it, and the shadder o' the sky,
And the shadder o' the buzzard as he goes a-lazin' by;
Shadder o' the pizen-vines, and shadder o' the trees—
And I purt' nigh said the shadder o' the sunshine and the
      breeze!
Well—I never seen the ocean ner I never seen the sea:
On the banks o' Deer Crick's grand enough fer me!

On the banks o' Deer Crick—mil'd er two from town—
'Long up where the mill-race comes a-loafin' down,—
Like to git up in there—'mongst the sycamores—
And watch the worter at the dam, a-frothin' as she pours:
Crawl out on some old log, with my hook and line,
Where the fish is jes' so thick you kin see 'em shine
As they flicker round yer bait, *coaxin'* you to jerk,
Tel yer tired ketchin' of 'em, mighty nigh, as *work!*

On the banks o' Deer Crick!—Allus my delight
Jes' to be around there—take it day er night!—
Watch the snipes and killdees foolin' half the day
Er these-'ere little worter-bugs skootin' ever' way!—
Snake-feeders glancin' round, er dartin' out o' sight;
And dewfall, and bullfrogs, and lightnin'-bugs at
    night—
Stars up through the tree-tops—er in the crick below,—
And smell o' mussrat through the dark clean from the old
    by-o!

Er take a tromp, some Sund'y, say, 'way up to "John-
    son's Hole,"
And find where he's had a fire, and hid his fishin'-pole:
Have yer "dog-leg" with ye, and yer pipe and "cut-and-
    dry"—
Pocketful o' corn-bread, and slug er two o' rye,—
Soak yer hide in sunshine and waller in the shade—
Like the Good Book tells us—"where there're none to
    make afraid!"
Well!—I never seen the ocean ner I never seen the sea—
On the banks o' Deer Crick's grand enough fer me!

OLD MAN'S NURSERY RHYME

IN the jolly winters
   Of the long-ago,
     It was not so cold as now—
Oh! No! No!
Then, as I remember,
   Snowballs to eat
Were as good as apples now,
   And every bit as sweet!

In the jolly winters
   Of the dead-and-gone,
Bub was warm as summer,
   With his red mitts on,—
Just in his little waist-
   And-pants all together,
Who ever heard him growl
   About cold weather?

In the jolly winters
    Of the long-ago—
Was it *half* so cold as now?
    Oh! No! No!
Who caught his death o' cold,
    Making prints of men
Flat-backed in snow that now's
    Twice as cold again?

In the jolly winters
    Of the dead-and-gone,
Startin' out rabbit huntin'—
    Early as the dawn,—
Who ever froze his fingers,
    Ears, heels, or toes,—
Or'd 'a' cared if he had?
    Nobody knows!

Nights by the kitchen stove,
    Shellin' white and red
Corn in the skillet, and
    Sleepin' four abed!
Ah! the jolly winters
    Of the long-ago!
We were not as old as now—
    Oh! No! No!

THE MULBERRY TREE

O, IT'S many's the scenes which is dear to my
mind
As I think of my childhood so long left be-
hind;
The home of my birth, with its old puncheon-floor,
And the bright morning-glorys that growed round the
door;
The warped clabboard roof whare the rain it run off
Into streams of sweet dreams as I laid in the loft,
Countin' all of the joys that was dearest to me,
And a-thinkin' the most of the mulberry tree.

And to-day as I dream, with both eyes wide-awake,
I can see the old tree, and its limbs as they shake,
And the long purple berries that rained on the ground
Whare the pastur' was bald whare we trommpt it around.
And again, peekin' up through the thick leafy shade,
I can see the glad smiles of the friends when I strayed
With my little bare feet from my own mother's knee
To foller them off to the mulberry tree.

Leanin' up in the forks, I can see the old rail,
And the boy climbin' up it, claw, tooth, and toe-nail,
And in fancy can hear, as he spits on his hands,
The ring of his laugh and the rip of his pants.
But that rail led to glory, as certin and shore
As I'll never climb thare by that rout' any more—
What was all the green lauruls of Fame unto me,
With my brows in the boughs of the mulberry tree!

Then it's who can fergit the old mulberry tree
That he knowed in the days when his thoughts was as
      free
As the flutterin' wings of the birds that flew out
Of the tall wavin' tops as the boys come about?
O, a crowd of my memories, laughin' and gay,
Is a-climbin' the fence of that pastur' to-day,
And a-pantin' with joy, as us boys ust to be,
They go racin' acrost fer the mulberry tree.